FINDING MEANING

A TEENAGER'S GUIDE TO LIFE IN THE 21ST CENTURY

By

Frank Nieman

Created Equal:

Meaning in the Twenty-first Century

Contents

Introduction
Part I: The Search
    i. The Beginning
    ii. Order
    iii. The Questions
    iv. Law
    v. Things
    vi. The Humans
        a. Their Coming
        b. On Method and Ideas
        c. The Great Leap in Complication
        d. Love and Persons
        e. Maturing Into Love
    vii. Someone
    viii.. Spirituality
    ix. Spiritual Development
        a. The Human Substrate
        b. Spiritual Growth

    x. Meaning
    xi. Death and Life
    xii. Conclusion
Part II. Jesus of Nazareth
Part III. Method
Part IV. Humans Alone
Summary

CREATED EQUAL

MEANING IN THE TWENTY-FIRST CENTURY

INTRODUCTION

"They told me I was born." The English essayist, Gilbert Keith Chesterton, opened his autobiography with some facts about the fundamental helplessness of being a human. We become part of the incredible mystery of life with absolutely nothing to say about our arrival. We have no say in when, where, or to whom we are born. As we grow up into our part of the world, we are bombarded with endless amounts of information about how we are to conduct ourselves if we are to prosper, or even survive. With childlike simplicity, for we are children, we accept this growing volume of vital lore and live more or less according to it. If we are born among head-hunters, we hunt heads and are happy doing it. If we are born among northern Eskimos, we hunt seals. If we are born among Wall Street bankers, we devise loans. We live and die fairly close to the mores and manners into which we are born.

Ultimately, however, life cannot be summed up so simply. Almost every life is lived as if it had a specific purpose. Sometimes a purpose can be expressed in words, sometimes it is not clear. Hedonists are a possible example. If one watches them day in and day out, they try to cram as much pleasure into their lives as they can. They might even work very hard, but when they collect their pay, they buy more pleasure. Other lives, like Spartans, Misers, and Monks, are almost diametrically opposed to Hedonists. But they are quite different from one another since each has a different reason for not indulging deeply in pleasure. Still others live to have Power. They invest great effort into gaining political office or corporate control. Over the long haul, most persons find special direction that gives meaning to their lives.

Giving direction to one's life is part of becoming a completely mature adult. The thought put into this effort usually depends upon the amount of leisure and opportunity each person has. To be born into a Third World country gives one little time for choosing a way to live. Getting shelter, clothing, and enough to eat can take up all of the time and energy of a whole family.

At the other extreme is the "upper class" of a First World country. There, if they so choose, leisure is what life is about. The burdens and stresses of life may be relieved by servants and money, and life is able to become whatever one wishes. In such an environment, one may find oneself forty years old, never having been gainfully employed, yet still amidst only the finest things of life.

Humankind has amassed a great deal of information about itself, especially in the last one hundred years, that suggests life has within it a pattern, and even a direction. Life can hold a special meaning for each person. Finding the pointers to meaning and the meaning itself is our purpose here.

The basic discoveries of modern science as well as its limitations are respected here. For example, Evolution is recognized as more than a theory. Evolution, at least in its root sense of "coming forth" (*evolo*) or of "unrolling" (*evolvo*) has been proven, even though some applications of classical Darwinism have been seriously challenged. What seems to be missing in the literature of the past century and a half, with the notable exception of Pierre Teilhard de Chardin, are the implications of what evolution means for human life. The stages of development of the galaxies and the solar systems have been outlined. The geological phases the Earth traversed on its way to becoming a life-supporting planet can be found in geological textbooks. The development of living things and the order of their progression has been slowly unearthed and made available to all able to read.

However, in the process of all of this investigation and discovery, it seems as if diffidence, and sometimes even hostility, has developed toward anyone asking about meaning on a grand scale. Since "meaning" is neither measurable nor observable with laboratory equipment, it appeared to be "unscientific" and, thus, an illegitimate question. But questions about meaning are real, legitimate, and their answers are as demonstrable as are the description of the atom itself.

Hence, the basic question is one of meaning. What, if anything, is life all about? Do we have a rational foundation for choosing what we do with our lives? Most of the people of the world – even those confined to subsistence living – have some ability to give their lives a distinctive meaning. Within the mystery of coming to be a person on planet Earth, and apart from the admonitions of persons of faith, does any evidence exist for choosing, to the extent possible, to live one's life in one way rather than another? Does it really matter what we do with our lives once we find ourselves here?

The method of this search is rational. The presumption is that the universe is orderly and reasonable. The search is not any way contrary to things of faith, but merely seeks to find reasonable understanding that lies under faith. If faith and reason are at odds, one must give way for the Order of the universe demands it.

Plato, in <u>The Apology</u>, tells us that Socrates was of the opinion that, "The unexamined life is not worth living." In the final analysis, if we search reasonably and carefully, we may discover that human life is not only a mystery, but an adventure of epic proportions for every single human being.

PART I: THE SEARCH

i. The Beginning

Once so very, very long ago that it could only be called Before-Time, in a place so vast and dark and empty that it could only be called Nothing-At-All, an explosion happened. Scientists, looking back, say it was by any measurement the most powerful explosion that could ever be. Many strange things besides the force of the explosion have been discovered. For one, the material for everything we can see or know, Particles, in as yet unknown forms or "pieces" probably smaller than a bit of light, were contained in the explosion. The bits, perhaps of a now defunct form of light,[1] needed only to be reorganized and the rocks and sand, the blazing sun, the moon and stars, the plants, the animals, the people would all emerge. No one looking at the blast would ever have been able to fathom what would come from it. The burst could only be called The Incomprehensible Explosion. Some scientists, more inclined to slang, call it, "The Big Bang."

ii. Order

As soon as this Incomprehensible Explosion occurred, another strange and wonderful thing happened. One would expect that chaos would occur,

---
[1] Magueijo, João, <u>Faster Than the Speed of Light: The Story of a Scientific Speculation</u>. Perseus Publishing: Cambridge, Massachusetts, 2003.

with things flying about in haphazard directions – but it didn't! Within an instant (scientists call that a "nanosecond", or 1/1,000,000,000 of a second), the streaking, hurling, tumbling Particles were gripped by forces that, taken all together, could only be called Order. Absolutely nothing escaped Order. The Particles pushed and pulled on each other in such a way that patterns were quickly formed, swirls and whirls, cartwheels and curls, with centers pulling in and edges pulling out. Most of them glowed brightly but some became dark, and after only a few billion years there were many different groupings with different shapes and sizes and properties. They were so diverse and continuously changing that they could only be called Things.

At first, the Things formed from the Incomprehensible Explosion were relatively limited in kinds and numbers, but they kept interacting with the Particles and other Things, pushing and pulling according to the Order in and around them. Sometimes they would gather into vast quantities and, in the intense gathering pressure, the intense pressure of pushing and pulling, they would make a totally new Thing.

The Order in them seemed to be endless. Just when a new blob or element, a new world or sun would be formed, and it would look like a completed thing, it would do something new, like collapse or explode, expand or contract. Another new Thing – or even many new Things – would come to be formed. Such systematic, and often repetitious happenings occurred that an observer – one who did not know that the material involved was what we call "inanimate matter" – might think that the Things and other particles had a mind of their own and knew what they were doing!

We know when and where the Incomprehensible Explosion occurred because we know the speed of light and that the stuff flying away from the explosion was, as it were, "streaking" away. We can tell "away" from "towards" by the streaks. Streaking can be caused by lingering impressions on the eye caused by the great speed of the moving object, or by real Particles being left behind by the moving object. "Streaking" can sometimes be merely a change in color over the passage of time. Either way, the streaks are always behind. By noting the different location and the "newer" color, speed and direction can be calculated. Scientists refer to some of this cosmic streaking as "The Red Shift Effect."

The Incomprehensible Explosion and Before-Time are now some 13.7 billion years behind us, but the incredible force and Order continue.[2] Still tumbling away from the place of Nothing-At-All, we can look back in time. Though the Things we see have long ago faded away, they are so far away that we can look back and examine them. Suns that have long ago gone out can look to us like they are just coming into existence because their distance from us is so great.

If this does not make sense think of it in another way. Suppose that light and sound travel only one foot every second. Suppose you are at one end of a football field that is the usual 100 yards, or 300 feet, long. Suppose at the other end a man comes out, puts a tin can on the ground, puts a firecracker under it, and lights the firecracker. The explosion of the firecracker sends the can high into the air. When it comes down, the man collects the can and walks away. The whole business is finished in three minutes.

You, however, are 300 feet away and the light and sound from the man with the firecracker do not get to you for 300 seconds, or five minutes. Thus, by the time the light hits your eyes and you see the man walk out with

---

[2] In early 2003, a NASA space probe sent back results enabling accurate calculations of the age of the cosmos at the 13.7 billion year figure, to within an error range of only 1%. A picture of the Cosmos was also obtained of the way it appeared only 380,000 years after the Big Bang.

the firecracker and tin can, he had already left for home two minutes before! So it is when you look into space. Real light travels more than 186,000 miles per second, but the distances are so vast that we can watch the making of a star that has already burned itself out. With a really good telescope, like the Hubble telescope, we can look back in time and see Things being made by the Incomprehensible Explosion and the Order in it.

The different Things, occurring from the stuff of the Incomprehensible Explosion and the Order pushing and pulling within them, startle us with their variety and beauty. The many precious stones, often formed in the furnace-hearts of our molten planet, dazzle us. The various elements confound us with the complexity of their structures and the infinitesimal size of their parts. Their peculiar properties, from sluggish inertness to a radioactivity so dangerous that a brief contact with it can mean death, all seem to be made up of a multiplicity of incredibly tiny particles rearranged almost imperceptibly by the Order within Things.

We people of the Earth, rather recent arrivals upon the cosmic scene, have been carefully examining Things and their Order for a few centuries with telescopes and microscopes, with experiments, measurements, and tests, and have learned to repeat a few of the procedures. We have also begun to identify a small number of the simpler laws from which Order seems to operate. These basic pushings and pullings, interactings and reactings, are all carefully measured and give rise to the sciences of Physics, Chemistry, and "the Natural Sciences." Even the inner activities and basic pushing and pulling of people are being observed, measured and re-measured, and these are called "the Social Sciences."

iii. The Questions

But some questions <u>all</u> of us ask, ones not answered in the sciences, are the questions we want to deal with here. They are "The Why? Questions." Is life just a stage, as the English literary giant, William Shakespeare, said, "…full of sound and fury, signifying nothing"?[3] Why are we here? Are we going anywhere? Are we part of a cosmic joke, a meaningless illusion – or a profound mystery? What's it all about, if anything, anyway? Where can we start?

We can certainly agree that these are very serious questions which, if meaning exists, we would be a little foolish not to try to answer them. To be given a free cruise, say, on the Inside Passage to Alaska and spend all ones time between ones stateroom and the dining room, never going out on the deck to view the mountains or the sea, never listening to an explanation of the area, flora, and fauna, would be foolish. To be given a trip across Canada on the Transcontinental Railroad and never look out the windows or visit the Vistadome Car would be a great waste. To not get out of the car to look into the Grand Canyon because, "I've seen it on TV" is disingenuous. Life is a free trip in a sensational universe and a thoughtful investigation of ones surroundings will reveal some startling information – about oneself. Not to investigate may result in our dying without knowing why we have lived!

Perhaps we can find some answers by examining the long process that brought us here. The atom can help us to discover our meaning. The atom, to put it simply, was discovered from the effects it had, even though the atom was too small to be seen, even by a microscope. Some scientists kept

---

[3] <u>Macbeth</u>, V,5: "Out, out, brief candle! Life's but a walking shadow; a poor player, that struts and frets his hour upon the stage, and then is heard no more; it is a tale told by an idiot, full of sound and fury, signifying nothing."

noticing that lines appeared on some photographic plates lying about in a laboratory. But, when some very rare material was taken from the laboratory, the lines did not appear. When the material was brought back, the lines reappeared. "Lines do not make themselves," the scientists sagely observed. "This material is strangely active and is making the lines," they next said. Then, after trying to determine what was missing from the active material, they said, "Very tiny 'bits' from the active material are making the lines – and they are so small nothing could possibly be smaller. We will give them a name that means, 'uncuttable' [ατομος]. We will call them 'atoms'." More and more experiments were designed and more and more became known about the atoms, including the fact that they contained many smaller parts and were not "uncuttable" – though it was too late to change the name.

But some scientists were skeptical. They said, "We have never seen these atoms, so they are theoretical. This is the 'Atomic Theory', not the 'Atomic Fact'." Other scientists, like Albert Einstein, said, "The atom may only be a theory, but if you bombard it and split it open, stand way back!" They followed his advice and, when they split the atom in the first atomic bomb, they stood way back and were glad they did. After that, more and more scientists talked about the atoms, and hardly anyone mentioned the "Atomic Theory" any more. A very few still do, but they are the same people who insist the Earth is flat!

In the last century, many new experiments have revealed more and more about atoms. For example, we know that only about one hundred and twenty exist and we call them "elements." Everything in the known universe seems to be made up of these few atoms. Each of these atoms is immensely different from all the others. Some are gathered tightly by their

Order and tremendous effort is needed to break them apart, and some are so loosely gathered that they tend to turn into other Things even as they come into existence. Moreover, every time we examine these atoms and their peculiar gatherings with other atoms we seem to find wonderful new Things that help our lives become better. Were the leaders of the world to induce their countries to cooperate in a search for useful new things, they would probably find plenty of profitable work for everyone in the world to do for years and years to come.

More and more struck by the Order in things, we can examine the unfolding of the universe over the last 13.7 billion years and find out something about its purpose and direction. Like the "streaking" of a moving galaxy that tells us which way it is heading, we may be able to tell where <u>we, as human beings,</u> are headed, and why!

iv. Law

The Law of Gathering seemed to be a basic rule of Order. The particles sent flying by the Incomprehensible Explosion started to move towards each other, and no particle just went off by itself unrelated to other particles. If any human beings had been able to view the Incomprehensible Explosion, they would probably not have reacted to it like they would to a regular "explosion" – which is to duck! – but more like they react to one of those starbursts found in large fireworks displays. They would ooh and aah at the obvious patterns unfolding, just the way astronomers have always done when they look through telescopes.

While the Laws operating in the Big Bang were inexorable, Time spent to accomplish their purposes did not seem to be a serious consideration. The time-line of the early developments after the Bang have been worked out in some detail, and modern Science tells us that it took 380,000 years for things to get cooled off enough for the formation of the simplest atoms, like Hydrogen and Helium. Before that, if they tried to form, they just flew back apart.[4] Billions of years had to pass by before even the possibilities for life could be present. Even when a place for life, like our Earth, is formed, the emergence of life takes billions of years of cooling and rearranging, all by the same inexorable laws.

Another aspect of the Law of Gathering became evident when the particles, already complicated in themselves, gathered and became even more complicated, eventually forming totally different, more complicated Things. Some of the simpler things could be predicted from the particles gathering or from the speed of their gathering or the size of their gathering, but most Things seemed to form for no reason yet discovered. Nonetheless, all the particles seemed to get more complex the more they gathered so that a Law of Complicating was quite noticeable. The longer the particles and Things were around and interacting, the more Things happened, and the more complicated some of the newest Things became.

Like the discovery of the linear direction of galaxies, a form of "Streaking" has been discovered about Things. If the Red Shift Effect tells us which linear direction a galaxy is going, the process of complication in the development of things from one kind or stage to another gives us a structural "direction" for Things. If particles are simpler than atoms, then particles precede atoms. If non-living is simpler than living, then living follows non-living. If touch is more basic than seeing, and must precede it in the development of things, then to see is to an "advance" over merely to touch.

---

[4] Michio Kaku, Parallel Worlds: A Journey Through Creation, Higher Dimensions, and the Future of the Cosmos. Anchor Books: New York, 2005, p.293.

Because of Order and the Laws that express it, "Producing more complicated Things" is certainly one direction in which the Cosmos is going. In addition, perhaps a reason exists for this since "Becoming More Complicated" by itself is quite unsatisfactory as an ultimate answer. <u>Why</u> are things becoming more complicated? Are there any defining characteristics to the complicating that would give more clues to the direction?

When one watches for the first time an archer shooting at a bulls-eye, one does not take long before one says, "He is trying to hit the very center every time." When one watches the direction of the universe unfolding and sees a pattern of complicated emerging, to ask, "What's it doing?" is a good and sensible question. Indeed, answering the archer question with, "He is just shooting arrows" has an incomplete ring to it once the target is hung up and the progress towards accuracy is observed.

Someone might say, "I am not the least bit interested in anyone shooting arrows." However, that is not proof that the arrow shooting is not purposive. Some people are not the least bit interested in finding an ultimate meaning to life, but that does not mean it doesn't have one. Carefully observing regular target practice with a bow might reveal information – even about the bowman. For example, observing a bow and carefully examining it could even reveal the very dimensions of the bowman, right down to a measure of his strength. Perhaps we can find meaning in the way we came about.

v. Things

Cosmic Particles could always be found, but the longer that seemingly-simple dust-like stuff gathered and the greater the quantities of it that pushed and pulled on themselves, the more likely some explosion would occur. When it did, not only rocks and shaped chunks, some bigger than our whole

Earth, would happen, but the whole range of our known elements would be produced. Fires would start – not the kind you find in your fireplace, but atomic ones like those that make up our Sun. A disinterested observer at the time of the origin of the Earth, would probably come to this conclusion about what the Incomprehensible Explosion had been doing: "It is making galaxies." Looking closer the same observer might even say, "It is making planets" since they appear to come after galaxies and suns.

An immense variety of things, going in the single direction of becoming more complex under the Order expressed in the Laws of Gathering and Complicating, made up the largely immeasurable twinkling and sparkling Universe we see when looking up into the night sky. But far more was happening. Looking down and around ourselves had its own wonderful surprises.

The Earth probably began as a planet 4.530 billion years ago as a fiery blob circling an even more fiery Sun.[5] As the ages passed, the Earth cooled and, in the cooled rocks and the formed Things that lay about on it and in it, the story of its own ever-growing complexity lay hidden. Looking at this world and its process, from gathered and packed Things glowing with heat to the world we live in today, reveals another Law of Order.

Just as the Incomprehensible Explosion was not random, so the cooling Earth did not just have bits of everything chaotically mixed and haphazardly strewed about, but it cooled in neat layers or zones. These zones, called the Bathysphere, Lithosphere, Hydrosphere, Atmosphere, and Stratosphere, had each its own properties and differences. They all combined to make a haven

---

[5] In August of 2002, a team of scientists in Germany and a team of scientists at Harvard University arrived at the 4.530- billion-years figure independently.

for, and provide the conditions and materials for, Life! The Order of the five spheres had cooperated to make a sixth called, "The Biosphere."

This formation is tremendously significant in our search for meaning. What we find around us is a movement of Order which piles up whole geologic systems, each seemingly quite independent of one another. Yet, after they are in place, another movement of Order occurs which makes use of all of the independent systems to effect a single new kind of Thing! In other words, we could examine each zone individually, and in great depth, and never have a clue about any of the forms of life which Order, using all the zones together, brings forth

. We could look at them all together just before the first living thing emerges and probably not be able to predict the marvel of even a one-celled animal like an amoeba. Yet, once having seen life appear, we know that a "direction", an "order" has been at work throughout the construction of the spheres. After the forms of life appear, we say, "Of course, this life form fits right in here!" What this tells us is that Order is not simply within things, or in any one thing in particular, but in the Whole of Things, quite outside of them all, yet in each one. Otherwise, whole spheres of Order would not mesh with other whole spheres – at least not in such an Orderly manner.[6]

When the stuff of the Incomprehensible Explosion began gathering, apparently many of the items that we called The Elements happened first. The elemental atoms were already immensely complicated, having many inside particles which made them different from one another. Hydrogen was very different from Oxygen, though both were Things that wafted about easily compared to Iron and Gold. The former were called "gasses" and the

---

[6] The anthropologist and philosopher, Gregory Bateson, would call all this order, "Mind", and with obvious good reason.

latter "metals." But even the two gasses, always subject to the laws of Gathering, would come together and Complicate and, according to the Order governing them, would make the Thing called "Water." Strangely, water was a liquid, not a gas, and why two such gasses should make water is even now lost in the complexity of Order. Similarly, the Complication, "Sodium", is a metal with an interesting Order of Gathering and quite poisonous if ingested. It sits calmly in air (another very interesting complexity) but gets immediately involved in fire and explosions when dropped in water. It reveals itself as a rather restless Thing. If it gathers and complicates with Chlorine, another gas quite deadly for people to breathe, it becomes Table Salt and we sprinkle it on our food!

How a deadly metal and a deadly gas amalgamate to become something that makes our food taste better is also lost, except in terms that leave more questions than answers, in the unfathomable mystery of Order. Every day another treatise is produced by a scientist in a university explaining new discoveries in Order and in Complexity, but more new questions seem to present themselves as mysteries are solved. We do not want to say that a really good explanation of Order is beyond our comprehension, but we can feel confident in saying that the cooperation of all people of the world working together for a very long time would be needed to figure it out. As already mentioned above, that would give everyone in the world, if educated properly, something worthwhile to do, perhaps instead of wars and such.

Looking closely at what happens when sodium and chlorine get together, we must say that they lose their original center. They lose the place that makes them a single thing and from whence comes their properties of injuring lungs or catching on fire in water. They become a new Thing with a new center that has the property, for one, of making food tasty. They lose their centers and get a new, more complicated center that, if properly attacked, can be broken down and the old centers made to take over again. The Law of Gathering is nuanced by a Law of Centering.

When two or more atoms join together to form a different Thing, with a new center, the new Thing is called a Molecule. Careful scientists have created names for all the known, different processes and their effects, but these properties and reactions are not the focus of our concern here. We merely note that the new complexities are stable <u>unities</u>. We discover that the more complicated a Thing is, the more wonderful are the properties that come from its new center, from sealing wax to strawberry jam made with tomatoes and without strawberries.

The first hint of a vast Law of Centering emerges. An ever wider examination of the Earth's Gathering and Complicating, a Complicating that moved from molten dust through elements to living plants, animals and people, finds the Law of Centering steadily operating -- a third basic Law of Everything. "Centering" moves ordered unity from one being to another! It "reorders" a Thing, perhaps by reorganizing its infinitesimal, inmost parts that no one has ever detected by any experiment.

Just as the Laws of Order describe how the stuff of the Incomprehensible Explosion forms the Elements, and the Elements form molecules like water and table salt, so the same laws appear to describe the formation of living things. As more complicated molecules gathered with other complicated molecules around them, some appeared to become so centered that all of the gathered, different molecules began to work together for the benefit of the new Center, the New Thing.

Not every molecule that bumped into the New Thing enjoyed the benefit of the Gathering. Some molecules were dissolved or dismembered by the

17

center of Order or New Thing. Some of the gathered molecules lost their own center, their own individuality, and were subsumed under the Center and direction of the New Thing.

The new complexity moved from being called a "Thing", with a center and a complex set of properties, to a new, higher complexity that was obviously centered as One Thing, but so complicatedly and actively gathered with the world around it, that it was called a "<u>Living</u> Thing."[7]

The internal and mysterious Order that drives the very complicated things formed from the particles of the Universe is, to now, quite unexplainable. The Process of complicating caused by Order goes by the general name of "Evolution." The tiny, unseen elements of the Process have inspired an entirely new science recently called "Nanoscience", and it deals with the study of structures on the scale of 1 to 100 nanometers. A nanometer is 1/1,000,000,000 meter and a human hair is around 50,000 nanometers across.[8] Atoms appear to have many internal parts that we have not fathomed at all, and they are busy forming many things that we are just finding a little about.

We cannot, as a result of these findings, say that a living thing, so obviously different from a non-living thing, needs something new added

---

[7] In his excellent challenge to over-simplified theories of evolution, Michel Behe notes, "No one has ever explained in detailed, scientific fashion how mutation and natural selection could build the complex, intricate [biochemical] structures discussed in this book." Agreed, they have not. But, with Behe we note that these complexities have <u>appeared</u>, and appeared <u>regularly</u>, and the universe is of orderly design. Without simply avowing Evolution, especially simple Evolution, we add that a certain timely order and increasing complexity of the unfolding design constitutes, like the data gathered from watching the bowman at target practice, real evidence about its origin and Originator. Cf. Behe, Michael J., <u>Darwin's Black Box: The Biochemical Challenge to Evolution</u>. The Free Press: New York, 1996, p.176.

[8] The main building blocks of the Universe appear to be sub-microscopic, and even sub-atomic. The search for a unified theory of the Whole, an ultimate Einsteinian synthesis, is thwarted by our lack of knowledge of the number, kinds, and complexities of the particles and/or waves inside atoms. The "simple" compounding of two atoms to make one molecule totally "other" than either of its components warns us of the fundamental mystery of the makeup of things. Today, a whole range of Dark Matter and Dark Energy is complicating the analysis.

beyond the Things that gathered to make it up. We simply do not know enough about the inner complexity of things.[9] If Sodium and Chlorine have, within the mystery that is each one of them, the property to come together to make table salt, perhaps they could have in their respective mysteries the properties to help make a Living Thing. Simply put, the origin of living things may be explained with the laws we have thus far enunciated and, while admitting that we know little of their infinitesimal makeup, we must not, without clear new evidence, posit new processes or laws to account for their coming into existence.

As noted, the reason one complexity was called "Living" and another, just a little less complicated, was not called "Living" was that the living had a peculiar unity of a variety of activities interacting with the world around it and emanating from a single center. "Life" appears to be simply a variety of relationships among various kinds of highly complex matter.

Similarly, the difference between "Living Thing" and "Conscious Living Thing" appears to be a matter of complexity. The common element in conscious living things, providing us with a clue to Going Somewhere, appears to be what we call "Mind" or "Thought" and, under some circumstances, "Knowledge." However, the longer science examined the world of the living, the more it became convinced that <u>all living things are conscious or, as some said, have "Mind."</u>

A blade of grass, trying to grow, may run into a rock in its way. It acts differently from the same blade of grass next to it that did not run into the rock. It seemed to become "aware" of the rock and act differently, using a myriad of its parts to go forward or aside in a different manner. True, the

---

[9] The methodological rule is quite ancient that one ought not add things to solve a problem where what is already present has not been proven to be insufficient for an explanation. It appears in medieval manuals as: "Beings ought not be multiplied without necessity" (Entia non sunt multiplicanda sine necessitate.)

higher animals, when they burrow into a rock, react immediately and very quickly. People might test for rock and not bother to dig in a rocky place at all. But the differences among the grass and animals and people are not in being "aware." All are "aware" but some are only what we might call "pre-conscious." They differ in the speed, complexity, and intensity of their consciousness and the reactive vitality of their "center." If one poked a dog, the whole dog reacted and one might even be bitten. If one cut a tree, nothing seemed to happen. It was deemed "Not conscious." However, observed over time, the whole tree became involved in the healing of the cut, and grew over the scar, sometimes so completely the scar was invisible.

But speed, complexity, and intensity are all functions of a quantitative rather than a qualitative response, and do not introduce anything really new. Order, when producing a living thing, appears merely to be rearranging the original stuff of the Incomprehensible Explosion, perhaps some of the "nano-parts" deep inside it.

If nothing new has been added to the Universe during the period of the movement of some Things to Conscious Living Things, then Conscious Life has "evolved." Everything, even in the direction of the non-living, contains the elements of consciousness! Conscious life could easily be but an intensification of the same mysterious "gathering" activity that exists in the most common elements. Their centers, like sodium encountering water, "know" what to do when they encounter the right conditions, and what not to do in others. [10]

---

[10] This phenomenon is has been startlingly observed in the genes of DNA. The same "optic" gene of a mouse, without which the mouse will not develop its shining dark eyes, will cause the multifaceted, insect eyes of a fruit fly to develop when transferred to the that creature's DNA. Submicroscopic complexity is immense.

A going Somewhere, as it were, in the unfolding of the Universe, 13.7 billion years in the doing, seems obvious. But equally clear is the fact that Gathering can be complicated beyond our wildest imagination and we may never come to know the total complexity of the microscopic, or the macroscopic, structure of anything.

What increasingly seems to be clear is that the Laws of Everything work very consistently. When conditions are right, atoms form molecules – but always the same atoms form the same molecules under the same conditions. Highly complex molecules would then seem, under the right conditions, to have formed tiny living things – and the same complex molecules would do so under the same conditions, unfailingly. When the hominids (human-like animals) of many thousands of years ago were situated interactively with their environment, they grew in complication and began thinking.[11] Complexity proceeds steadily over time.

One of the most interesting aspects of the development of different Things on the Earth is its time-line. A very accurate method of dating has been found within the structure and contents of Things. Large, new Things usually take a very long time to make. Our human genetic structure is 99% the same as a Chimpanzee, but that one percent appears to have taken two million years to develop. Millions and millions of years are involved in evolution. We now know that Dinosaurs were long gone before any people appeared. More generally, simpler Things are, as far as such matters can be determined, <u>always</u> found before more complex Things.

Moreover, in evolutionary theory, the complex things come directly out of the simpler things even as the simpler thing tries to maintain itself. If a

---

[11] For one view, cf., Jaynes, Julian, <u>The Origin of Consciousness in the Breakdown of the Bicameral Mind</u>. Boston: Houghton Mifflin Co., 1990.

simple thing multiplies itself long enough, spreads itself around long enough, its members will eventually react somewhere in its environment to produce a new more complicated Thing of its own kind.

The new Thing will spread out as far as it can into its own environment and repeat the process. The original, simpler form will either maintain itself or die out. This process is called by the scientists who maintain it, "Orthogenesis." The whole, overall process of Things developing into more complicated Things is called "Evolution" but, because of the weakness of its more simplistic forms of expression, we prefer names like "Designed" or "Orderly" Unfolding.[12]

Just as direction can arise without addition to the original stuff, so too the directional movement of the known Universe from particulate matter to people can be envisioned as a consequence of the same laws that existed in the Incomprehensible Explosion. As Things happened because of the Gathering, Centering, and Complicating of the first particles, so the Living Things and the Thinking Things can be seen to be emerging from the same laws.

The same laws of Order made the new living thing restless, internally developmental, and expressive of a newly formed self. The same laws drove the simple living thing into becoming a more complex living thing by gathering with other Things and Living Things. The same law of Centering caused the newly formed, more complex, living things to retain a single, but now more complex center that eventually became a brain.

---

[12] Some persons, especially when reading sacred texts literally, have tried to dispute these claims. However, by the time they have learned enough science to dispute the claims, most find themselves in agreement with them! The evidence for some kind of designed unfolding, so big a pile that no one can climb over it, is solidly established. Perhaps more wonderfully, they also learn that their sacred texts remain their sacred texts when God is recognized as supportive of the Order of the Process. We will deal with this again later.

The "inside" of Things is immense in number and infinitesimal in size. (Some bacteria, not the smallest of Living Things, large in comparison to many non-living things, and immense when compared to atoms, are found to be 1/5000 of a millimeter in length.) Order's Laws of Gathering and Complicating and Centering, carried out at that tiny level millions of years ago, produced a complication which could "live." A new center, unlike even the most complicated molecule, began to have properties of self-actualization. Philosophers, even ancient ones, startled by its unifying grasp, call it "the soul." Developed to their extreme, these same properties would in one species, the humans, include self-awareness.

At the level of the Incomprehensible Explosion, particles moved towards each other by the same law of Gathering, expressed in a very simple form as gravity. Now, intensified in the complex molecule, it drove the latter to complicate into the Living Thing. Centers that go from being the nuclei of atoms, to the nuclei of single-celled animals, to the brains of persons, are all developed by the same orderly progression we see in the panorama of Incomprehensible Explosion to Earth. As the explorer Humboldt discovered, the order of climate and living things appearing at the various levels from the bottom of a mountain in the tropics to its top in the snow is the same as found from the Equator of the whole of Earth to its Poles. Order and Law are universal.

vi. The Humans
a. Their Coming

The story of the ascent of Humankind from the simplest life-forms to the present can be found in the clues that remain in the world of rocks and fossils. After scientists learned how to calculate, through carbon-dating, how long different things had been in existence, a pattern showed itself. True to the law of Complicating, simple forms of life were older than any complex forms, and the most complex form of all, humans, appeared among the very latest Things produced.

Among the simple living forms, a complexity was found beyond any of the non-living forms, and a great length of time elapsed before their arrival. Next, these simple living forms turned into more complex forms by Gathering and Centering. Barely living unities themselves, they apparently maintained their own lives but cooperated with other simple forms to do something that none could do by itself, like all wagging their tails, or *flagellae*, in unison to create a current that will feed them all. They were "many" with one life and, by only a small step of Centering, became one thing with complex parts. These new unities became the first forms of a single life with many highly complex functions.

The older ones seemed to have the center of their organization spread upon the outside, and the newer, more complicated ones highly focused on the inside. Thus, the Law of Centering went hand in hand with the Law of Gathering. The more complicated the living thing, the more "inside" its center of direction, its "brain", became. Governed by the Order inside its parts (its "orthogenetic character") and driven by its environment, each Thing gathered with the world around it, and became more Complicated and more Centered in its life. Size did not seem to be a major factor. Huge dinosaurs came and went millions of years before much smaller humans appeared. But, the humans were much more complicated and centered.

Humans were so complicated and centered that they became the first product of the Biosphere to be able to think in a systematic and abstract manner, and to look back, discover, and analyze the source from which they came, the Incomprehensible Explosion. They appear to be alone among the products to have calculated the great distance of almost 14 billion years they have traveled.

Looking at the night sky and analyzing its motions, its light, and its activities, the humans noticed that its Laws of Order were the same as those on the Earth. Their speeds and distances could be clearly calculated like earthly bodies. Going Somewhere, whatever the goal, seemed to grip the entire Universe.

The emerging story of the human journey is both simple and immensely complex. The movement is simple because only a few laws seem to drive the whole process. It is immensely complex because of the variety of the elements involved, the things already existing, and their own previous history of complicating and centering. Like the Biosphere that requires five other spheres even to come into existence, human beings required their stage to be set by millions of years spent in its construction, and thousands of species to come and go.

Important to mention in passing here is a dictum of science. That dictum says, "Just because a thing takes a long time to form does not mean that it forms by accident."

What seems to emerge from investigation is that groups of living things, each with a few hundred simple parts (but an untold number of tiny components of each part), gather because of ideal conditions for their continued life. They appear to unite around their mutual continuance but, at the same time, to struggle with one another for their individual development through dominance. Uniting against groups of other living things trying to occupy their niche in the world, they vie with them for the most nurturing spot within the same niche. Order, working through their parts and the components of their parts, seems to drive them towards dominance of their environment and perfection within their species. No real "failures" occur. Even species that "failed" to survive apparently contributed to the competitive striving of other species and, of course, to the food chain.

Whole groups of animals lost their place in existence to more aggressive species. The latter were usually those with more complex adaptations. Creatures, faster because of longer legs, stayed around longer until their predators become as swift as they were – often by growing longer legs. Creatures with sight <u>and</u> hearing dominated those with only one or the other sense. What evolved is a highly complex world, the Biosphere.

From its beginning the Biosphere was marvelously balanced. Every niche became filled with the creatures who could occupy that environment and, with enough to eat and room to reproduce, continue to thrive in it. If the creatures in the niches gathered and complicated at any time, the new emergent species tried successfully or unsuccessfully to extend its niche, ultimately to continue and develop, or fail. Knowledgeable people in this area indicate that what Order was really tending towards was a species that could live in any niche, like the humans who are found both in tropical grass huts and in igloos.

The amount of time involved in this process is staggering to the mind, and even to the imagination. One aid to thinking about this is to stop for a moment and think about how long the year just past took, and then think a bit slowly about how many one million are. The lineage of human beings begins with a lizard in Asia and ends with an erect human in Africa *three hundred million years* later, and in a direct, verifiable genetic line. Scientists tell us that we parted from our nearest relative in the animal kingdom, the chimpanzee, nearly two million years ago. The history is in our DNA cells and cannot be otherwise. We are the product of a Gathering-for-Survival by a long series of species, and a Competing-for-Dominance to improve each succeeding species. In our present form, we arrived on the scene as self-aware beings, *homo sapiens sapiens*, only about sixty thousand years ago.

b. Some Necessary Talk of Method and Ideas

Just as discussion itself did not happen until creatures arrived who were able to discuss things, so all possible dimensions of existence beyond the first four, Length, Breadth, Height, and Time, went unnoticed also. With the humans, and their pursuit of knowledge, understanding, and love, came such a startling awareness of new things and possibilities that we must digress in our search and talk about ideas and methods.

Although we are merely passengers on this great odyssey, people could not help but notice that, if one comes from a place and then always goes through a definite process to get to a new place, one might be able to tell where, if anywhere, one is going beyond where one is presently. In addition, at least by searching for an answer to the question, "Where to?", one might obtain a hint of an answer to "Why?", the basic question of this book.

Because, for three hundred years, the Scientific Method has dominated western thought, we have become accustomed to expressing our discoveries in terms of scientific legalese. When we discover the time-line of complicating from non-living to living, we refer to the Law of Complicating, and also express that law like it was <u>inside</u> the Thing complicating. An important observation here for the student of these matters would be to note that *no proof exists that the complicating occurs from the inside.* Order, in some form we do not know of, could be reaching into the Things and changing them or they could be "pulled", like a magnet, from the outside. This may not be so, but we do not have proof, and that is important to recognize. True truth seekers must be very careful about their language.

We also need to clarify some important terms, and to remind ourselves of some venerable wisdom, known as *philosophia perennis*, that has never been disproved by modern science. Following those ancient traditions, we could call the guiding Center of a living thing its "soul." This is not to be confused with its nerve center or brain, but is that "x" that directs all of the parts of the living thing. Usually, it uses the brain to retain its notions, and uses the nerve impulses to collect information and to transmit its directives. It may even be in the brain, but not of any three-dimensional thing known to be there. In a pet dog, it is the closest thing to being "Rover" found in that beast, more so than his nose or his toes, and certainly more so than his hair that he leaves about wherever he goes.

Until recently, the "soul" of anything less complex than the human was thought to be some quantitative, inner part. Now it is considered "Immaterial", simply a way of existing that is not measurable or observable, but inferred from effects. Also, "immaterial" could be a dimension of corporeality that is either too minute to be found, or of a dimension containing neither length, nor width, nor depth. Scientists now think a dozen "dimensions" might exist because so many effects have not found explanations.[13]

Ideas, or the meaning of ideas, are always immaterial. They *are*, but, by definition, are beyond the scope of so-called "Natural Science." However intimately they are related to our nerve impulses in our brains, they are not those impulses, but "carried" by them. Since we use them every day, and

---
[13] Magueijo, Faster..., p.144

they are more important to us than many measurable things, we do not want to define them out of existence. As some have noted, ideas cause armies to march and history to change. They are very important existents.

The same venerable philosophy tells us *spiritual* things exist. We do not usually refer to things these days as "spiritual", but "of another dimension", one that simply defies discovery by The Scientific Method. A "spiritual" soul, indeed, a "spiritual" anything, may survive the death or dissolution of a body that it directs or informs. However, the soul of animals, and perhaps humans who have not attained a spiritual state, could remain an "x" called Rover, Tom, Mary, or Harry. They may even be "immaterial", but dependent upon a three dimensional thing for existence. Disturb excessively the body of anything not spiritual and, poof! – the soul is gone. The human, spiritual soul is not measurable or observable except by its effects, and, according to philosophers, remains with all of its history transferred to its spiritual, that is, non-three-dimensional form, after the body dies. Maybe it even goes outside of the fourth dimension, time.

A few candidates have recently appeared to answer the question, 'What is the soul made of?' The best one is 'a combination of Dark Matter and Dark Energy.' In August of 2006, scientists finally proved the existence of Dark Matter and Dark Energy from observing a cosmic explosion in a distant galaxy. This "stuff" is called "Dark" not because it is black in color, but because it is unable to be detected by any known scienfitic method. It cannot be seen, felt, heard, touched, or smelled. It can be so tiny that it is measured in nanometers, if at all. A nanometer, as mentioned above, is 1/1,000,000,000 meters.

This new phenomenon may have immense power that we know nothing about. Like the atom, with its incredibly bottled forces, Dark Matter/Dark

Energy may contain the answer to the mystery of the stuff of the human soul, and the souls of animals. It may explain, finally, why nothing that existed in a living thing seems to be missing after it dies. The soul is "Dark."

The discovery of Dark Matter and Energy turned the world of the Natural Sciences upside-down. Writing before the final proof of its existence, the renowned physicist, Michio Kaku, said,

> "After thousands of painstaking experiments, scientists concluded that the universe was basically made up of about a hundred different types of atoms, arranged in an orderly periodic chart, beginning with hydrogen. This forms the basis of modern chemistry and is, in fact, taught in every high school science class. The WMAP [Wilkinson Microwave Anisotrophy Probe] has demolished that belief.... ...23 percent of the universe is made of a strange, undetermined substance called dark matter...." [14]

"Soul" and all such terms are used to give words to phenomena that are understood to exist, but for which no adequate explanation is given. We all know that abstractions exist, but they cannot possibly be material things. They must exist in immaterial "souls" or they could not be. But they *are*. We know, as will be noted elsewhere, that $\sqrt{-1}$ is the useful number called "*i*", but it is completely irrational. It *is*, but if it were a material thing, even a nerve impulse, it would be useless. Without the understanding of this Other World, we can never get beyond the rather narrow, though quite useful, boundaries of modern science. Poetry simply cannot be reduced to nerve impulses, not even to quantum physics.

This notion of a "meaning" is widely misunderstood in the modern world. Quite serious persons will even claim that robots will soon be able to

---

[14] Kaku, Michio, <u>Parallel Worlds: A Journey Through Creation, Higher Dimensions, and the Future of the Cosmos</u>. Random House: New York, 2005, pp.11-12.

think. This is a gross misunderstanding of understanding. If robots ever think, they will be produced by nanotechnology that has discovered what in humans comprises their souls and enables them to abstract.

We have no evidence that "meanings", like poetry or "*i*", have ever been produced in animals less complex than humans. We are obliged, as investigators of our own gift of life and its meaning, to account for poetry, love, abstract thought, and a myriad of other items that modern physics, chemistry, and other sciences simply leave dangling, along with our seminal question, "Why are we?"

Humans: c. The Great Leap in Complication

Returning to our saga, we note that at first we were certainly not immediately "cultured" people, but a quite ignorant bunch of primitives. We probably immediately were *able* to be kind and gentle with our offspring, notice beauty, and out-think every lesser critter around us. However, the struggle to survive probably caused us to imitate the beasts around us and act more beastly than human. We had the potential to become what some are today, thoughtful, concerned persons, caring for those around us, developing tools and methods of survival that would create leisure and, with it, time to think. Writing, reading, scientific development, and the ultimate overcoming of our natural tendencies to solve problems by aggression and violence were only distant possibilities, but they were real possibilities.[15]

Like all of the more complex species, the individuals of our newly-developed kind gathered together for survival every time some other species

---

[15] For the theologically inclined reader, we note that most mainstream Christian thought has held that this emergence was by a new, special cosmic act. These sages seem to know what God is capable of doing and not doing in a manner beyond this author's comprehension. Their conclusion is not unanimous. See the conclusions of Robert North, S.J. (Teilhard and the Creation of the Soul. Bruce: Milwaukee, 1967), and the remarks of Karl Rahner, S.J., in his Introduction to that work, especially those on "concursus" (*passim*).

wanted the same space we had. We developed complex brains that finally assured us of complete control of our first solid niche, a small area in Southern Africa. The story is still in our genes.

These immediate ancestors, *homo sapiens*, slowly grew in dominance and in numbers. The need for space or provisions probably was a basic impulse for them to begin to wander, but from the moment they began thinking, we may not rule out their wandering as simply a matter of curiosity! This was a really new kind of animal, one that could choose to do what it wanted instead of being driven only by instincts.

Starting from that small area in Africa, our ancestors emigrated about the Earth until they had gone into every corner of it. Moving north to what became known as The Fertile Crescent, they entered Asia. Over generations they moved along the coasts of Southern Asia to Australia. They also traveled to mid-Asia and, splitting in many directions, they populated Western Asia and Europe, Eastern Asia, and finally the Americas. Again, the story is in our genes, though only recently able to be read.[16]

We developed agriculture and ceased our nomadic search for food. We grew in numbers and overwhelming dominance by virtue of our brains – until we began to bump into others of the same species. A crisis ensued.

Millions of years of honing skills for competitive survival and internal dominance had the expected results. If you bump into a neighboring settlement with fields and flocks, compete for them! Take them if you can! Those attacked would not be happy and their instincts for competition would suggest that they lick their wounds, gather, and attack back. Man as warrior emerged as naturally as man as hunter/gatherer.

---

[16] Wells, Spencer, <u>Journey of Man: The Story of the Human Species</u>. PBS Home Video: Alexandria, Virginia, 2003.

Moreover, as reproducing the species is as important as feeding the species, the dominating impulse of the stronger males is to predate for females, and preferred females at that. Sexual predation by males became as much a factor in competition as predation for food and other good stuff. The relative success of some ancient rulers (and a few modern ones!) can be easily discovered simply by counting the number of his wives and children.

Motives for predatory behavior apparently soon surpassed simple survival – space, food, and reproduction –in favor of looting and slave-gathering. "Civilizations" came and went with little progress, leaving behind only the vestiges of beautiful, ruined cities and artifacts.[17] Human kind had reached a point of "development" where its own inner drives for survival were beginning to threaten the very survival it sought.

Meanwhile, even as humankind was perfecting itself as a dominant warrior and predator, other developments were taking place -- inside. Moving about the Earth and encountering different kinds of environment, kinds of food, and other humans, the still-developing people were continually honing their complication. Abstract thought and free will, were fine-tuned into the mathematics for great building projects, developed religions, kinds of government, and philosophical theories. Some even asked, "Why are we?"

The problems persisted, but we kept learning. We began to discover that we could choose to compete and try to dominate, following the basic instincts that had served us so well, or we could choose to gather together, discuss alternatives, and share equally. The latter was the way of survival and growth as strongly suggested by our newest thoughts and our brightest

---

[17] For examples, the Seven Wonders of the Ancient World.

successes. Our directive instincts were coming into conflict with our directive thoughts – and now we had to choose!

The source of our information about what we humans did with ourselves when we emerged from brutes is both in the artifacts and monuments that survive from our distant past and, after writing was invented, in written history. But the informative fact about our development as creatures produced by Order, referred to as "the genetic line", has only recently emerged. As already noted, the history of the development of any person can be found in the cells that make her or him up. Who I am and from whom I came to be begotten are present in my "life code", my "DNA." Each and every person's DNA is unique. For the first time in the history of American jurisprudence a man was proven to be the murderer of another man whose body was never found! Enough blood was found to convince authorities that the person whose blood it was must be dead. Then, by examining the cells of the Mother and Brother of a missing man, they could tell from their DNA that the blood found had to belong to the missing Son or Brother. Each blood cell of the victim told the authorities the story of his parentage and also much about his relatives.

In the ova of all women and the sperm of all man, the special and unique code of all their parts is present. And they pass it along. We have come to be from a marvelous process that has taken almost fourteen billion years!

No one has seen DNA. But, almost on a daily basis, criminals are convicted because they "left DNA" at the scene of the crime. What the Prosecutor points to as evidence is a "DNA Profile." The latter is a picture, constructed into the form of a chart, of <u>reactions</u> by chemicals and light to material left at a crime. It is not a picture of DNA, but of the <u>effects</u> of DNA, unique to every person but identical twins. However, nothing avails the criminal who tries to argue, "No one has ever seen DNA, so how do you know I was there?" Much can be learned from "effects."

We noted that another interesting fact about DNA is that each generation puts its own mark into the genetic code. The genetic code both causes and records forever the unique set of characteristics of each human being. By the appearance of, say, a very peculiar mark added a long time ago, the lineage from that person on can be traced with precision. Similarly, like the use of the Red Shift Effect, the lineage can also be traced backwards, even when the offspring keep moving about. Using the opportunity to trace lineage of people backwards, contemporary scientists have proven that we, *homo sapiens sapiens*, all are one human family coming from a small group of Bushmen in Southern Africa 50,000 to 60,000 years ago. Some of our people are still there. What is found in their blood is now found in ours. Even the Australian aborigines and the Chukchi nomads of northeastern Mongolia bear in their blood the unmistakable marks of the same tribe of Bushmen that ours does.

The Americas were populated by a group of Mongolian nomads just 12,000 years ago. After wandering for over 25,000 years before getting to the Americas, they needed only 800 years to reach the bottom of South America.[18] In a word, no such reality as "race" exists, unless you want to refer to the one "human race." Though some of us are quite ethnically different, we are <u>all</u> cousins! Scientists are quickly gathering all the information they can about this fabulous human journey because, with modern transportation able to move people around the globe in hours, the story of the travel of the genes will be lost forever in the mixtures of the next couple of generations.

---

[18] Wells, Spencer, <u>Journey of Man</u>.

Humans: d. Love and Persons

Reflective self-awareness is the ability to know what one knows and, at the same time, know that one is knowing. Together with abstract thinking, it has given humans, the latest known members of the evolutionary process, a powerful tool. Information, often abstracted and otherwise generalized, is gathered, codified, utilized, formed into sciences, and passed along. The Earth grows "smaller" with instantaneous communications. Computers do, in seconds, calculations that took weeks, or even years, for a human to perform only a few decades ago.

With our ancient history of competition and predatory behavior, these new facilities could have been very dangerous. Fortunately for humankind, another advance, following close on the heels of free choice and reflective self-awareness, has provided a means to save the situation. This advance was the development of the inherent capacity of humankind to choose to care for fellow humans beyond their own self-interest, and even to give up their lives for others. We call this capacity, "Love."

Because of the unfortunate history of English words, we must immediately digress here for a moment and say clearly that "love" as used here, and everywhere else in this book, has <u>nothing</u> to do sex or with "falling in love" or "being in love." "Falling in love" is a temporary, emotional regression to a childish attitude that all the problems of ones life can be cured by the person "loved", just like ones Mother did in ones early childhood. It is probably a clever trick of Order to induce primitive humans to reproduce. As we have matured as a species, this infatuation has become a great burden on those who marry because of it and then discover it is temporary. They are then faced with the need to love in the proper sense, that is, to decide to live for the welfare of the beloved, and with the beloved, for "our" mutual good. That so many do is some kind of attestation to the human spirit.

True love is a decision, not an emotion. True love, however accompanied by feelings, is expressed by what one decides to do, not merely what one feels like doing.[19]

Apparently emerging out of the law of Gathering, thoughtful people could, in complete freedom, help and care for others when they received absolutely nothing for their efforts. They often cherished others rather naturally when the occasion was their own offspring and their own families. However, they appeared reluctant to exercise this way of acting for non-family members or strangers – or enemies. But Love was growing.

This power, Love, advanced humankind like competition, but far less destructively, and love was soon recognized as highly significant in the development of people. Unloved, people were just very skillful animals. Loved, they could be transformed into dynamic persons, transforming themselves and all around them. Love, seemingly a product of the faculty of "choice" or "will" in humans, instigated the people who were loved to work together and achieve things far beyond what people could do by themselves, even in competition.

Love is very mysterious and the words, "seemingly a product of human Choice", are used advisedly. Just as humans do not know where each thought comes from or how exactly one moves from one thought to another,

---

[19]The need to understand this distinction today, with the world's astronomical divorce rate, is desperate. No one, to this author's knowledge, has given a better description of the difference between the "love" of "falling in love" and true "love" than the psychiatrist, M. Scott Peck. Cf., The Road Less Traveled: A New Psychology of Love, Traditional Values and Spiritual Growth. Simon & Shuster: New York, 1978. Esp. cf. pp.84-91, "Falling in Love."

so, too, the power of love seems to be an even more mysterious matter. Rather than the force of human will, love appears more an instance of letting the force of Gathering work inside one, and not getting in its way.

Similarly, we may not take credit for the forces that move us from infancy to adulthood – they just operate by Law, and we grow and mature, reaping the benefit. In ordinary circumstances, we may not take credit for great insights or discoveries because the natural action of the human mind sorts and gathers collected evidence, often while we are asleep! We may certainly take credit if we do stupid things, like smoke cigarettes or drink excessive amounts of alcoholic beverages. But, may we take credit for the refusal to do these very same things? The good we do appears to be the result of not getting in the way of the great Order that produced us, and the bad we do our stubborn insistence on certain dis-Orderly courses of action.

The real truth is we arrived here from an awe-inspiring explosion a long time ago, and with no help from ourselves. Love comes naturally from the law of Gathering, but some people hate anyway. Hatred seems to be some kind of rationalization of dominance, itself already disorderly behavior. Love can also be called "being responsible" or "responsibility." That is, we "respond", or give a "yes" answer to the force of Order within us, instead of showing a "lack of responsibility", failing to respond to Order.

Love is the ultimate Gathering and most intense Centering found coming from the Incomprehensible Explosion. Its ability to cause humans to lay down their life, to love, either individually in crisis or collectively in defense of ones beloved country or people, is the highest of cosmic activities yet making an appearance. As the first particles reached out for each other and gathered in to make the first Things, often at the cost of their own independent existence, so the complex, macromolecules, impelled by Order, interacted with the world around them to make living things. Infinitely more complex, human beings, under the urgings of Order and acting freely, reach out to one another to form societies and cultures.

However, with all these choices, the world's quality has not moved "forward." "Progress", in the sense of the forward movement of the Cosmos as evident in the direction of the last 13.7 billion years, is towards Gathering and Developing, not scattering and disintegrating. Almost from the beginning, and certainly from the beginning of recorded history, some leaders, perhaps not noticing that the universe brought them forth as a free gift, and not different from any other human on the face of the Earth, became predators upon other members of the human family.[20] They created so-called products of advancement, like cross-bow guns, catapults, atomic weapons, armed rockets, and supersonic bombers, and make the world less safe than it was before these "advances."[21]

Countries going to war always claim "self-defense", of course, and "National Security." The ancient Romans always described their wars as "Defensive", even at the height of their imperialism. But almost no war has ever been fought that has not been proven to be unnecessary, albeit centuries might elapse before the proof can be clearly seen.[22] A war here and there may have been necessary, but, as historians usually point out later, only because a series of previous human blunders finally left no way out. Some leaders or people, reaching deep into their primitive past for their survival

---

[20] Sages do not argue about human equality – it is, as the most famous statement about it says, "self-evident." Cf. the United States, "Declaration of Independence", second paragraph, "We hold these truths to be self-evident, that all men are created equal…with unalienable rights…."

[21] To stay perfectly clear about the "they" here, we must add the observation of Albert Alligator in that great, old comic strip, "Pogo", "We have met the enemy and they is us!"

[22] Interestingly, the late Pope John Paul II apologized to the world for the Roman Catholic Church's leadership or other involvements in the Crusades, a series of "holy" wars taking place from 1096 to 1291. They appeared right and just at the time they were pursued. After at least 700 years, they were finally seen as very bad choices.

drives, cause wars by treating others as if they did not share equally in the gift of life and the Earth. We humans seem to have a problem within us, at war with ourselves.

Knowledge, reflective self-awareness, and the ability to love would seem to be the tools that enable humans to attain the peak of their perfection. However, their ability to choose changed everything. If Things in the Universe prior to the human's coming were only what Order wanted to unfold, this new being, the human, would be different. The Universe where they existed would, in some important respects, become *what the humans wanted it to become*, whether towards greater perfection or away from it!

Two of the intellectual tools of Gathering would seem at first glance to cause people to reach out and relate to one another. However, any serious review of humankind's efforts at social progress would soon reveal that knowledge and self-awareness are neutral to mankind, able to hurt it as well as help it. Societies, even with large libraries and many universities, can be cruel, uncaring, and stupid. They can, even while they have many individuals who disagree with them, create large armies and march about stealing the wealth of others, armed both with weapons of war and reasons why their prey is not equal with them. They can formulate crude notions of God and sacrifice their citizens to this god. They can form and encourage clever institutions that prey upon the unwary as a means of enriching themselves. They can focus their energies on commerce – business – and waste their lives amassing things or money.[23]

The self-centeredness and greed of the immature is what a life of a thinking being can be – but not necessarily. When tempered by honest

---

[23] It is one thing to amass money for the sake of getting wealthy, and quite another to amass money for what good can be done with it. But even the latter is very risky. Money is not called the "Root of All Evil" for superficial reasons. For a more lengthy treatment of human folly, cf. <u>infra</u>, Part IV, "Man Alone", pp.133ff.

concern for others and a desire for the others' development and goodness, that is, when human living is tempered by Love, people become "persons."[24]

Seemingly endless possibilities then open up before them. What was a rational animal seeking power becomes a person seeking good for others. What was a human being piling up as many things as possible becomes a person making sure that everyone gets enough of what they need to develop their giftedness. Problem makers, with love, become problem solvers. Moreover, with the right kind of leaders, whole communities can become lovers.

With the wrong kind of leaders, whole communities talk about "other" people – the ones not agreeing with them or their aims – as "its", "things", first objectifying them, and then despising and using them. The step to eliminating them becomes easy as it was in the Nazi's elimination of Jews, Gypsies, the mentally retarded, and dissenting religious and political leaders.

When the majority of people within a society become persons of love, the prospects for that society are unlimited. Nurturing the gifts of all its citizens, as in that great American institution, the public school, the loving society always finds the gifted persons it needs for becoming ever more mature. Such a society will spend the majority of its resources on the very best facilities and teachers for its youth.

The basic reason for this widely-cast education of the young is because knowing where great giftedness, or any real giftedness, will show itself is impossible. The distribution process of Order is quite unknown. Love is the ultimately pragmatic action for a society to help itself. It will also carefully nourish, educate and monitor the health of even the most unwanted or

---

[24] We borrow the term from the popular usage that refers to some totally uncaring people – people without sympathy or empathy – as "non-persons."

neglected child. The perfectly natural anger and resentment of the unwanted and/or neglected child who, like ourselves, had no choice in the matter of where or to whom he or she was born, may be diffused by a caring society and a wholesome education. Moreover, that very child may be the one with the gifts especially needed next for the ever-progressing society.

The only way out of the grasp of those who do not love appears to be to love those same people. "A man convinced against his will is of the same opinion still," the old adage goes. Arguing does not seem to get anywhere – in fact, it seems to galvanize the opposite perspective. However, when one does something caring and friendly to the person who insults them, the possibility of their changing opens.

The effect is usually not immediate. People who want to settle all disputes by force do not take kindly to being loved. They get even more angry – for the moment. Then, when away from the scene and with time to think, they may become a little more loving. People nearly always change when they are loved by someone honestly trying to do them some good. For a few, unusually shattered in mind by surrounding dysfunction, some ostracizing and/or incarceration may be a necessity.

Extending the notion of love as curative beyond individuals to communities and states may provide a solution to many problems. When groups of people are angry, love suggests that those at whom the anger is directed do something kind for them. We are not talking about "Bread and Circuses" here. Those are mere cheap distractions. We mean food, clothing, shelter and, especially, education.

When nation states become bellicose, love suggests engaging them in dialogue and asking them why they are so angry. Offers to help them, in whatever matter they say is causing them to send suicide bombers or begin raising armies, seems to work best in the long run. Love and kindness, sometimes apparently fruitless, remain the odds-on favorites to produce positive results. Not to act thus, as we have stated before, is to be immature and, perhaps, evil.

Humans: e. Maturing Into Love

The process of moving from one's infancy to a person of loving concern is not automatic. However strong the natural forces of Order within a human being, apparently they are more or less easily frustrated by the individuals, or by others who disturb the maturation process. A very early disturbance seems to produce "non-persons", as noted above, humans with no feelings of sympathy or empathy. These may, at worst, grow to be serial killers. The brains of serial killers have been examined after they have been executed, and no physical differences from others have been found even in the most careful searches.[25] Experts say they probably missed getting needed, positive attention at a crucial point in their development, <u>and</u> received abuse instead. The abuse sometimes seems to "imprint" the abused. Evidence exists that this can even happen during their first year of life, during the second six months.

Many people simply live life in a more or less self-centered manner and the sum of their existence after life is fairly non-destructive. This latter condition seems to be the way the vast bulk of humanity lives unless they become transformed somewhere along the way.

Fear is no small element blocking the maturation of a person: 'I won't get what I need if I spend time and energy helping others.' Only a careful

---

[25] Eg. John Wayne Gacy of Chicago, who murdered at least thirty-three boys and young men. The examination of his brain was done by the same psychiatrist who had lengthy conversations with him before his execution, trying to determine his motives and how he became the way he did.

contemplation of the Order within will tell a person when he or she is neglecting honest self-needs or obligations to help others. Generally, though, one cannot love others too much. As the highest perfection of near fourteen billion years of unfolding, love in the form of unselfish deeds in the care of others would appear to be the one way in which humans might develop into a next higher stage, if any exists. Since to this very point a higher stage has always unfolded, we have no reason to think loving will not lead to Somewhere Else.

The reason for the need for transformation seems to be that the normal human being starts out totally self-centered and needy, and this infantile state is necessary for survival. Crying when one is hungry, sleepy, uncomfortable, and a myriad of other conditions is natural to infants. It gets them needed attention. If humans mature, they move from self-centeredness to being able to take care of themselves, even to move away from their parents and on their own. This, however, does not get them to true maturity. True maturity is arrived at when the person can take care of others, and do so without complaint, pay, or admiration. In other words, a human is mature when she or he becomes a "person." A person is a human who can love, and the process of becoming a person, except in rare instances, is by being loved and deciding to act the same way. The impetus for an act of love seems to come from within and then is accepted and fostered or rejected.[26]

The laws of Order do not automatically produce loving people, persons, but usually require the cooperation of at least one other person. Even having attained the status of a loving person does not, apparently, guarantee that one will maintain that status. Becoming a complete person takes a lifetime. One

---

[26] Persons of a theological bent would say, 'That impetus is a grace, a gift from God.' Depending on their notion of man as "depraved" or "deprived", they will refine this statement further saying either that grace takes over the base human, or grace aids the somewhat fallen human. Either way, grace is necessary.

scholar noted, "… from the instant of the union of the gametes [the sperm and ovum, conception] there is present a single, unified being and operation toward the goal of complete 'personhood' which is never really finished until death."[27] We would add, "…if even then." The experts on the subject say that, if one does not progress, become more loving, one regresses. The opposite of the serial killer is the Mother Theresa. The opposite of focusing life on self-indulgence is the total dedication of one's days to the love and relief of suffering people.

If loving is the highest status a human can reach, then the basic challenge of life is to love; who is loving and who is being loved is not the point. We all need love to come to maturity, and need to love to be mature. From such a perspective, the answer to our basic question, "Why are we?", emerges as, "To love one another."

One thing that makes maturing difficult is the comfort that the normal human being finds in any given phase of life. Born to be self-centered in order to survive, a child physically and mentally grows naturally, step by step, towards maturity. But, after early childhood, any given step might require some element of the child's free cooperation. The child sometimes resists giving up the "free ride" of being waited upon hand and foot, and does not embrace becoming more self-responsible. The child fails, maybe only a little, to mature. All of us have these failures and our maturation depends upon us facing these failures, perhaps again and again, until we overcome them and move on. Moreover, these failures can be caused by the

---

[27] North, Robert, Teilhard .., p.255. North is reluctant to admit a formal difference between mere "people" and "persons." He states, "There is no biological or metaphysical reasons for postulating *different* forms to preside over successive phases of that unified operation." We agree with our former professor but must also account, in some fundamental way, for the enigmatic, almost robotic, lives of so-called "non-persons." The Christian Scriptures have an interesting, plausible, and simple explanation: "They are possessed."

parents "spoiling" the child, which is treating it in such a manner that its moving ahead is impeded. When this happens, Order seems to take over. Events in life challenge or invite the child to move on, and the child more or less cooperates. Order seems to desire everyone's ultimate maturity.

Simply stated, recovery from failure is progress, and sometimes great progress. The middle-aged human is a more or less loving human being – one more or less contributing to the Gathering, Centering, and Complexity of the human race. Order is always within each and every human being and accounts for all of the mysteries of each life – where it might want to go, what it might want to think about, who it might want to meet – but <u>never</u> what it decides.

Of course, no reference is made to this Order by people unaware of the Order present within them.[28] No "listening" is done – that prayerful goal in the teachings of all great religions. The result is that what is chosen is what the individual has become habituated to choosing. Such people make loving choices according to their development, or failure of development, in loving habits. At best, they live according to the highest development of the ones who raised them or the heroes they have chosen – without any conscious reference to the meaning of life. Order is there, but not consciously recognized. If asked, "What do you think life is all about?" they speak haltingly and appear confused.

The operational Order for humans is like that present as instinct in non-reasoning animals. The instinct that causes the robin to build its strong, elaborate nest from mud and wisps of grass and straw is the expression of the Order within it. This internal order does not vanish in human beings.

---

[28] Persons involved in religion have an advantage in this matter because they believe in a personal God as the One ordering everything.

Nursing at the breast is obviously instinctive. But as the human matures, instinct gradually changes from a driving force to the offering of possibilities for choice. The proper Order for any situation, even if only as the choice to do nothing at all, is always available to the maturing human.

One of the more obvious problems for a maturing person is the choosing of the most beneficent act, which we might call "good", over what is merely "pleasant." Pleasure is wonderfully immediate and, as a feeling, can almost overwhelm the one faced with a choice. Not unlike violence, its repetitive sharing causes it to grow in its virulence, not its satisfaction or containment. How many young people have become pregnant or caused a pregnancy and destroyed years of their lives because they "felt" what they were doing was "great"? Pleasure is in the body; joy in the mind and heart. Pleasure comes from sensation, joy from love and goodness. They are different and sometimes in opposition.

But, inside the normal person, the voice of Order is always there, if the person listens and distinguishes between the two. Getting in the habit of listening to the voice of Order is an enormous leap forward for a human being but, unlike growing in size or developing in shape, it does not appear to be automatic.

In summary, the Universe moves through the duration of its existence from the simple to the complex, from the scattered to the gathered, from the diffuse to the centered. If we but grant the incredible number and complexity of the very particles either coming from, or formed by, the Incomprehensible Explosion, we arrive from that startling event to ourselves with a minimum of interference. Order and its Laws impel us from there to here.

These Laws of Order equip us with a three-dimensional body of five senses and great usefulness. They add a set of powers of thinking in the concrete and the abstract, and endow us with free choice. They leave us with interesting pieces of evidence of our coming-to-be scattered both on our planet and in the heavens. This evidence indicates that we are pointed in the direction of Gathering, and that Love is the most potent of our powers. We examine all this with care and know one thing for an absolute certainty: human life is one big mysterious unfolding!

Even knowing the direction we are heading, we still do not know whether we have a serious drama or a farce. We do not know whether any plot exists. We do not know where we might end up, or why. But now, because of intelligence, those questions can be legitimately asked. After we humans are on the cosmic scene, all the players that we know of, from the simplest to the most complex, are in their places. The pre-production has been breath-taking in the meticulous care of its preparation. Can the curtain be lifted?

vii. Someone

We have never found any Order that did not have an Orderer. If we find a wristwatch in a swamp, we do not say, "What a strange thing nature has formed here." No, we say, "Somebody lost their watch." Neither do we expect Nature to do things in a haphazard or disorderly fashion. If we find the perfectly formed skeleton of a dinosaur in a rock in Utah, we do not say, "What very interesting shapes the cooling of the planet Earth has produced." No, we say, "A fabulous beast once lived here." <u>Nothing</u> ever happens randomly and Order appears <u>everywhere</u>![29]

---

[29] A pure scientist might say, "You can't prove that! Maybe they <u>are</u> just shapes from cooling." They are correct, of course. The beast has been 'demonstrated', not proven. Its existence is beyond a reasonable

Order is that vast and overarching control of the elements of the Incomprehensible Explosion, the Cosmic Grasp that made the galaxies, the stars and planets in them, and anything else that unfolded from them. Order is the Author of the laws that governed the production of things and the evolutionary process that gathered, centered, and complicated them.

Human beings can create chaos. We set off many explosions, especially in war. The result is a scattering of pieces everywhere, including humans and their parts, and they just lay there and disintegrate into their lower components. Never has one of our martial explosions resulted in a thing of beauty – much less worlds of beauty. The more we look at the results of the Incomprehensible Explosion, the more unlikely we can label it "accidental", "random", or "chaotic." "Unplanned", "Accidental" and such adjectives move into the realm of a primitive belief system.

The cosmos is going Somewhere. "Where" is not a matter of conjecture, but of wonder. Still to be asking "whether the universe has a direction" is like seeing a very high-tech car going down a beautifully constructed freeway in the middle of a vast desert and asking, "I wonder whether that car is going somewhere definite?" Of course it is! We just do not know where. We will look at some of these "High Tech" items again, under Death and Method, below.

We will say this now. "High-tech", like the composition of dinosaurs and humans coming from an explosion, <u>means</u> "Not Random." "Random", like scattered body parts after a military beachhead landing, means "any old way." Yes, the body parts obeyed the laws of gravity and other physical

---

doubt, not proven. To act as if the beast were a theory is to be "scientific", but not "reasonable." However, once the remains are scanned for DNA, the beast becomes scientific. The "atom" progressed similarly.

forces, so they end up on the ground and at calculable distances from one another depending directly upon the force applied to them. But that is not what we mean by "High Tech", and in the difference lays a vast world, the world of complicated design compared to accident.

In the result of random explosion, the Scene of Accident, the nature of the explosion is revealed: the sudden, uncontrolled release of force with parts landing wherever. In the result of the Incomprehensible Explosion, Our Scene, the nature of the explosion is revealed: a magnificently controlled release of force, a planned experiment. In the Scene of Accident, the intelligence of the exploder is revealed – someone who knows how, for example, to compound nitroglycerine, and to set it off. In Our Scene, the intelligence of the exploder is also revealed – an Intelligence that knows how to make humans emerge from an explosion.

This is a very important implication found in the effects of Order, namely, that Order, to produce intelligent beings, and especially persons, must be at least intelligent and loving, and undoubtedly super-intelligent and super-loving considering the complicated unfolding that produced humans. If Gathering and Centering produces "someone's", the Order behind it must <u>at least</u> be a "Someone."

Moreover, this process implies the relation of parenthood, "fatherhood" or "motherhood", between Order and the intelligent beings produced. If one begets people, one is a "parent." Finally, it means that the intelligent beings, having the same parent, are brothers and sisters to each other, down to the last human. We may set this inference along side the evidence of DNA showing that all humans are cousins, related by blood to one another.[30]

---

[30] Cf. Wells, Journey of Man.

At this point, as Someone and parenthood are implied, we need to recall the "Logic of Unfolding." The basic axiom involved is, "Nothing gives what it doesn't have." When intelligent humans "fall out" of an explosion, especially one that happened almost fourteen billion years ago, you are only being responsibly intelligent to ask the question, "How did intelligence get in there?" You may be being responsibly intelligent to say, "I don't know", but only after you have looked at the evidence.

However, you are not being responsibly intelligent to say, "Intelligence wasn't in the explosion" because, if it wasn't in some way *in* the explosion, it would not come out. You might be being responsibly intelligent by saying, "I don't know how intelligence came from such an explosion, but it did – so it was either in the explosion or in some form, beyond intelligence and containing intelligence, arranging the explosion." Some would say, "It was put in later." This, however, requires proof or, in the language of logic, it remains a *Petitio Principii* (Begging the Question). Where, when, who, and how must, then, all be answered.

We exist in a Scene that we might call the "Gift Scene", similar to what detectives might find in a "Crime Scene." We treat what is here as evidence. We know with absolute certainty that a time existed when no Earth was here, no Atmosphere or Hydrosphere, no Biosphere or living things, and more recently, no people. We know that all of these are now here. We know that, unless we leap to a creationist god who zaps in occasionally (a very strange god, indeed, given the evidence), we must say that making all of the items mentioned only requires the Gathering and intense Centering of what was there all along.

Therefore, being human, thinking, loving, must all be complex gatherings and intensifications of what was already there. While a fundamental bit of the Cosmos, present primarily as a subatomic particle, may not be much to look at by itself, it must contain the very substructure of our intelligence and the elements of our personhood, or these would not emerge in time and space. It must also be in direct contact with, and under the control of, such a powerful Orderer that it joins with other substructures to produce intelligence, love, and so on.

This call for an Orderer can be looked at another way. Look around yourself, your workplace, your bedroom, your living room. Have they ever been cleaned? If they are cleaner than they once were, a "cleaner" must have been there. Simply no order ever occurs without an orderer.

Producing anything does not necessarily mean that the Producer is similar to the produced in some sort of physical or structural way. If we produce works of art, they come from our ideas, but are not made of the stuff that ideas are made of. Rodin fashioned "The Thinker" out of clay and bronze, but what the clay represented, the art, is what Rodin has produced, not the clay or bronze medium.

When we note that humans must have come from "Someone" in order to be "someones", we draw very few conclusions about the "Someone." We do know that the attributes, "loving concern within an intelligent framework", must <u>at least</u> be present in the Someone, but in a quite unimaginable way. When we grasp the thoughtful perplexity of "The Thinker", we know that Rodin had to have a mind, and one that had experienced the perplexity of the human condition, even though all he has left us is a piece of statuary, modeled out of carefully arranged clay. If we came upon "The Thinker" even as unschooled savages, we would know immediately a great deal about Rodin, though we would not know his name. Similarly with the Someone.

When we see the "someones" all around us and know that, over time, they have come from the universe, we know some very interesting things about the Order producing them in the same way we know about Rodin, even though we have never met him. That is at once not very much and a very great deal, especially considering what a marvelous item a "mind" is. Similarly, when a single explosion produces humans, either in the explosion itself or behind it are all the attributes of humans, including love and personhood. This is at once very little and a great deal.

We might want to speculate, especially around the attributes that made humanoid animals into "someone's" but that would be mostly gratuitous. You can tell all kinds of things about a "mind", and, hence, something about Rodin, but if all you ever knew was "The Thinker" you would miss most of what is Rodin. Thomas Aquinas, seeking to explain us and our world, and arriving by argument at a Prime Mover, an Uncaused Cause, and an Independent Existent, was so boggled by trying to describe the attributes and powers that It would need to possess to produce Our Scene, he simply said, "This we call God."[31] This God is known by just about every human being under many different names, "Allah" and "The Great Spirit" included. As with Rodin, to know God's name is not to know very much about God.[32]

One aspect of this Order, naturally overlooked, is its obviousness. Marshall McLuan once said, "I don't know who discovered water, but I know it wasn't a fish." A quality of such overwhelming presence hangs

---

[31] Thomas Aquinas, <u>Summa Theologica</u>, I, q.2,a.3, cor. From here on "Someone", with a capital "S" and "God" are used interchangeably. The word "God" has generally been avoided in this treatise because, unfortunately, "God" carries a great deal of baggage with it, some of it quite unworthy of God.

[32] Aquinas, upon being praised near the end of his life for his brilliant writings about God said, "Videtur mihi sicut palea" – "They are so much straw." The theologian, John McKenzie, observed that Aquinas' word for "straw", "palea" more likely means the stuff you find on the floor of stables. Cf. McKenzie, John, <u>The Civilization of Christianity</u>. Thomas More Press: Chicago, 1986, p.23.

about the Order in the universe, extending from the tiniest movements to the movements of galaxies, that it becomes invisible to the person not looking for it. The greatest miracle, sages have noted, is that anything exists at all, much less that habitable worlds, people, and societies exist.

The Miracle of Now is, unfortunately, invisible to most people. And, once Now is taken for granted, the Miracle of Everything Else disappears. Like the alcoholic or incestuous family member who is known to all but never mentioned, called by psychologists, "The Elephant in the Living Room", the Miracle of Everything is ignored and comes even to be denied as a fact. On the other hand, as so much of life changes once the Elephant is acknowledged, so, too, life changes greatly with the recognition of the Miracle of Everything. Hope, Purpose, and for some, many unwanted Obligations leap into consciousness right along with the Miracle.

Only a little insight is necessary to realize that absolutely Nothing-At-All could <u>not</u> produce an Incomprehensible Explosion with Order in it. That vast, dark, and empty place that we named Nothing-At-All should probably have been called "Almost-Nothing-At-All." Truly no <u>Thing</u> existed there, but if no BEING, no "AM" were there, no explosion could have happened.

This must be true because we have found that Order <u>must</u> exist, and this Order can only be violated by freedom. We have summarized these insights of human investigation into things called "axioms" and one of them is, "From nothing, nothing comes." Since a Thing is one way of be-ing, maybe it would be better to say, "From non-being, being does not come." If no BE-ING existed at the moment before the Incomprehensible Explosion, no explosion would have come to "be" and no Order would have "been" throughout it. Explosions guided by Order do not make themselves, and the

Order – from which you and I came according to the Laws of Order -- can not make itself.

An Orderer must exist. And, because of the tremendous complexity, beauty and internal order of even the very tiniest of the things and be-ings that have come from the Incomprehensible Explosion, we usually call that Orderer, the Incomprehensible Explosion-Maker, "GOD."

Since humankind has been around on the Earth, God, or gods, or some representation of a powerful, intelligent Other or Others has been around. This universal acclaim of humans cannot be ignored in the search for meaning. It may be disproved or embraced, but to act like it has not always been there is not reasonable. We must look at the <u>whole</u> story.

This GOD, known like the atom from effects, especially the effects of the Incomprehensible Explosion, and especially effects like incredible power, beauty, and intelligent, loving beings found about the Universe, must be powerful beyond imaginable power, beautiful beyond imaginable beauty, and intelligent beyond imaginable intelligence. GOD, as the Author of the Incomprehensible Explosion, is Incomprehensible – far more than the atom.[33] At the same time, however, the <u>existence</u> of this God is at least as assured by reasonable argument as the existence of the atom. To belabor the point, one cannot say, "I know that atoms exist" and not say, "I know that God exists." More evidence exists for God than for atoms.

The usual reaction of anyone when they first realize the sort of entity GOD must be, and the necessity that this GOD must exist, is to experience a sense of great awe. Contained in the awe is a sense of recognition like, 'You

---

[33] We are forced to continue using the term "is." However, almost from the earliest philosophers who talk of God, God is considered "Beyond Being." We are too crude a kind of existent to be able to think about God the way God actually must be.

know, I always knew there had to be some reason for me and all these things being here.'

Some investigate the whole thing very carefully and, sometimes only after years of doing so, humbly acknowledge GOD. Others want to run and hide. Others get angry because they hate the thought that they owe Anyone anything, especially their very lives. Still others are angry because this Someone must be smarter than they are or, maybe, because they are not GOD themselves, and begin immediately to try to show that a mistake has somehow been made in the discussion that arrived at GOD. Some, realizing that their lives might need to be changed if GOD exists, do not want any changes and avoid talking about it – until they are old, or even dying.

Some profess themselves to be "atheists", that is, people who do not believe in GOD. They have an interesting belief-system but they are stuck with the being-from-nothing problem. Frequently, they proclaim, 'The Incomprehensible Explosion was the last in an infinite series of Incomprehensible Explosions,' as if moving the whole business back far enough into the dim past can eliminate the difficulty. Also, it does not solve the problem of intelligence in each explosion and, in general, when atheists are closely examined, they are discovered to have the most complicated of all belief systems.

A final group of persons says that, in spite of the tremendous Order in everything, it all happened by Chance. The great scientist, Albert Einstein, glancing about the immensely complicated and orderly cosmos around him, addressed this possibility saying, "The odds that the present Universe happened by chance are about the same as those of an unabridged dictionary resulting from an explosion in a print shop." No more need be said about Chance. One skeptic did press Einstein, asking, "Could those odds be calculated." Einstein looked pained, thought a bit, and said, "It would be a *very* large number."

As usual, one of the most notable things about humans is that they are free to do, and always free to think, whatever they want. However, a very interesting and frequent reaction by humans when they face the possibility of imminent death, is the acknowledgement of GOD. This phenomenon has given rise to a saying, "There are no atheists in foxholes."

As noted, God is discovered from effects found in the Universe. Usually, when looking at phenomena about us, we get so wrapped up in the display that we never think about from where or from Whom it came. Strange and wonderful things and events, especially in Nature, and especially in remote wilderness, startle us with Order and give us clues. An English poet, Gerard Manley Hopkins, in his poem, "God's Grandeur", was especially attentive to these phenomena:

> "The world is charged with the grandeur of God.
> It will flame out, like shining from shook foil;
> It gathers to a greatness like the ooze of oil
>   crushed."

We humans, and our complicated lives of gathering and centering, all seem to have come from a GOD of Order. And, as each new element of the unfolding story is read, the Orderer becomes ever more apparent and awesome. The Laws of Gathering, Complicating and Centering become recognized as the work of God. Reaching in and through the Incomprehensible Explosion and down through eons of time, the development of the Cosmos from simple Things to Persons-who-love is the work of God. "To be" becomes "to be held in existence by God." To become more and more gathered, complex, interior, is God visiting upon the

Universe God's own notion of development. "To love" is the ultimate expression of the Cosmos; "to love" is the nearest thing to God we have yet encountered. "To become" is "to grow toward and in love." The ultimate answer to "Why are we?" is, "We exist so that we might love."

Love is most interesting. It is selfless and caring. Its desire is for the other person, not the self. The first thought of a lover is for the other, the beloved. And, for persons who have taught us the extreme lengths of love, like Mother Theresa, the lover does not care what kind of person they love, or what condition they are in -- they are simply concerned, kind, and caring of them. It might even involve foregoing ones life for the other person or persons. As love is the nearest thing to God, the reason "why" humans exist is that God has decided to share life and beauty and, finally, love. We <u>are</u> because God shares. This is totally consistent with the Laws of Everything.

However, because love is a matter of personal freedom, the future is not assured. If the human race survives, our present day may be considered "primitive." But development will go in the direction of knowing and loving, the more gathered, complex, and centered ways of being, or it will not happen at all. This age may some day be considered barbaric because we charged our various cousins money to heal them from illness, or spent far more on the military weapons and military/industrial adventuring than on education. We will need to overcome these primitive tendencies. It is highly doubtful that we will be considered less barbaric if we go on developing more efficient atomic bombs, or more effective chemical and biological weapons. Moreover, if we go in that wrong direction, we may not exist at all.

If we are because of Someone Who Loves, and if our imitation of that is what is important for progress, then it is also important that we not be led by the stupidest, greediest, or most powerful and aggressive among us – albeit often decisive, self-assured, confidence-inspiring people. Rather, we need to be led by the gentlest, most generous, and self-effacing among us – the loving persons. What is important is that we not worry so much about spending our resources on people who do not appreciate what we are trying to do for them (so-called "welfare chiselers"). Rather, we should worry more about the vast warehouses filled with sophisticated arms and ammunition. They are even a greater waste since they have little, if any, possibility of producing good, and contain the distinct possibility of destroying all of us. As the present Dalai Lama observed recently, "Our prime purpose in this life is to help others. And, if you can't help them, at least don't hurt them."

Scientists who have discovered Intelligent Order and Unfolding Design in the universe, and even the reasonableness of a Someone, often remain reluctant to affirm the Design. While admittedly their reluctance to speak of "Someone" is solidly based in their methodology, their lack of enthusiasm to remind their audience that they have found Design can be tragic. Without Science in the context of Intelligent Design, the scientists tend to expend their efforts with little outcry and/or remorse – though not always – in the production of weapons of mass destruction.

Within Intelligent Design, a solid reason can be proffered for at least thinking twice before proceeding in such efforts. The one choosing to investigate by experiment is first of all a human being, equal with all the others and living within the same mystery. Then he or she, discovering gifts bestowed upon them without their having a thing to do with it, is a scientist. Science may be amoral, but scientists, like the rest of us, are either moral or immoral.

When we find that Someone exists, that GOD exists, our answers to our ultimate questions are overflowing with new possibilities, possibilities of which we never dreamed. If God is the Source of Loving, the ultimate human perfection, we have the delightful possibility that all the terrible things that sometimes happen in human life, from genocide and torture to untimely diseases and deaths, are ultimately in control of Someone who can make sure that <u>all</u> these things come out well in the long run. This alone can cause a huge sigh of relief, both for individuals, and the species collectively.

GOD not only makes the story all the more interesting, but provides the only reasonable explanation for the incredibly complicated, orderly phenomena that the various sciences find have brought us here. One of the more interesting possibilities is that, given that we are persons and given that God must have the attributes of "person", God and man might be able, in some way, to communicate with one another. With communication, perhaps we have a road to the answers we seek.

viii. Spirituality

Given that God is the source of Love, the Orderer of the Universe, and the Source of the Goodness, Beauty, and Perfection in it including minds and persons, the suggestion poses itself that human persons could relate to God in an interpersonal way. God is obviously very retiring. Capable of scattering galaxies, this Someone apparently prefers the quiet course of love when dealing with the Cosmos. Obviously capable of scaring any human being into a catatonic state merely by saying, "Hello!", God does not generally approach a human, even in the stillness of their inmost thoughts, without first being invited. Human beings' development of relations with the Someone has been long and slow in coming.

A personal connection between a human being and God is generally termed that person's "spirituality." Since spirituality is a relation, spirituality for each person is as unique as that person. When humans relate, they relate on the basis of what they know of each other. When God relates to humans, God must be understood to know the human in his or her entirety, "warts and all."

Once invited, God apparently enters very gradually into a human consciousness according to the invitation and capacity of the one asking to know the Someone. The spirituality of persons, then, ranges from ones of a vague, very tenuous (but real) relation to ones of an intense, always-living-in-the-presence-of-God relation. We call people with the intense kind, "mystics."

The force of Order working directly in a human life is one of those rare items of cosmic influence that we can verify. The fact of this influence is most clearly seen in the reforms of some of the lives of criminals and alcoholics. Faced with the chaos that they caused, both in their own lives and the lives of others, they are invited by people who have shared their experience to allow into their lives a Power higher than themselves.

They ask the Power to remove from them their own willfulness, the cause of their self-destruction. When fully engaged, they experience a new Power replacing their own wills and they are slowly extracted by that Power from their own chaos. Little in human life so dramatically bears witness to the personal Order in us than the daily occurrences of these wonders.

Spirituality becomes very important in all choices. Natural alternatives are always present, "to do the right thing" or "to do the wrong thing." We "listen" to the Someone so that we make the right decisions about what we are to choose to do. To do what is hateful, destructive, and such like, has been traditionally denominated as "evil", and to do what is helpful, constructive, and so on, as "good." In any choice we can go either way. [34]

If, as we determined above, the ultimate development of the Cosmos is a loving person, and if God is, indeed, described best by saying, "God is Love", a loving person is little different from a spiritual person. Then, too, difference between a spiritual act and an act of selfless love must be very small. In a choice to act lovingly, one makes a sort of God-like decision. When one consciously adverts to the Source of order, listens, and decides to act lovingly, one performs an act flowing from spirituality. The difference between a "loving" act and a "spiritual" act, at once very small and very significant, is that spiritual love is exercised <u>in conscious relation to God</u> as the Source of order, of ourselves, and of love.

The significance of the truly spiritual act, as opposed to a honest act of love in an unspiritual person, is understood in the special characteristics that accompany the former. The joy, peace, and confidence that flow from a spiritual act, especially one at the beginning of the spiritual journey, are very special. The joy is special because one is not only doing what one was made for, loving, but is conscious that <u>the very reason for being has been touched</u>.

Similarly, the peace that descends upon the human lover and spiritual lover is born of the natural calm that descends upon any person fulfilling an impulse to do what one is designed to do – to do what is best for another. But the spiritual person believes that following this impulse has an ultimate

---

[34] The literature on the subject of growth, usually "spiritual" growth, or "spiritual transformation", is vast. For a very popular summary, cf., M. Scott Peck<u>, Further Along the Road Less Traveled. The Unending Journey Toward Spiritual Growth</u>. Simon & Schuster: New York, 1993. Esp. "The Stages of Spiritual Growth", pp.119ff.

dimension, one of meeting the restlessness at the bottom of the heart, where the human is being called by the Voice of Order to listen. With continued "listening", that peace extends itself through the whole person, and such men and women slowly become known for their special calm. This is not at all true of the good, merely human lover.

Finally, confidence born from entering into a spirituality is unique to the spiritual person. Deeds that disturb, and even annoy people not guided by a spiritual life, by Order, are viewed by them as quite wrong, even mad. Truly spiritual persons, while carefully and eagerly consulting other persons with a spiritual life, pay little attention to the unspiritual, and vice versa. Each simply does not understand where the other is coming from.

Some persons' spirituality is quite weakly anchored in the relationship with God. These, unable clearly to "picture" or "personify" the Someone, find themselves relating – even talking – to the Truth/Beauty/ Intelligence that must somehow be under the beautiful world and cosmos that we live in. A certain wisdom exists in this approach since the Someone is certainly beyond human comprehension. Like Alcoholics Anonymous advises its members in the 12-Step Program, grasp whatever you can of the Power-Greater-Than-Yourself, "however you understand it", sincerely ask for help, and go from there. However vague, if the idea of the Someone is pure enough and the request is honest, the Someone will come to you. [35] Become willing to believe in the possibility that a Power greater than yourself might exist, and you <u>will</u> begin the road to a meaning-full life.

---

[35] You can understand God's dilemma in answering prayers of those who, for example, think God is a lion with a bird's head, or an old man with a beard. God answers the prayer and the one praying becomes forever convinced they have the correct notion of God. People who pray must have true notions of God. That having been said, what must be added is, 'God does whatever God knows is best for all.'

If you, the Reader, are reading this essay and some passage causes you to say, from some place deep inside, with a sense of deep conviction, "That's right!" or (heaven forbid), "That's wrong!", you are probably experiencing the Order within you. If you do not have a Spirituality, you are right on the verge of one. If you do not have a conscious Spirituality and suspect having been deliberately made by Someone, the best thing to do is to go to a quiet place and say, "Maker of all, thank you for this life. If You want me to live in a certain manner or to do anything in particular with my life, please show me the way." Or, after thanks say, "What can I do for You today?"

Be brief. Not entering into long monologues with Someone you don't know is usually the best approach. Then, listen! The Maker, who must at least be a Someone, will respond – not necessarily in spoken words or even startling thoughts, but you will know it when it happens. Then, voila! A personal Spirituality!

Another and, perhaps, simpler approach would be to go among people who have a developed prayer-life, a living spirituality. You can judge from their lives whether their spirituality is honest because, in keeping with the Order we have described, they will be very kind, forgiving, loving persons.

Everyone is open to God to the extent that they read from the deepest Source of their thoughts – they listen – and they interpret the events going on around them. In this life, all other attempts to contact God appear to be useless. People do not contact God in the active sense, but God is always in contact with them, and God contacts them, if God deems it appropriate, and especially if they have asked. God has so designed things, as it appears thus far, that humans are always "in contact" if they listen.[36] They can improve

---

[36] As a device that checks spelling in a computer can check an entire book in a split second, so apparently God, outside of, and maker of Time, can be present to every person in the universe *without using any time*!

their listening skills by learning various methods of contemplation and, for example, "Centering Prayer." Everyone should be, to some extent, a "contemplative" in this sense.

A word of caution – no one should ever say, "I am too busy for 'listening', for prayer and/or contemplation. That would be like saying, "I am too busy playing to eat." Not very much time will pass before such a one is unable to play. People generally seek happiness. Happiness (again, wealth, power, and pleasure are <u>not</u> meant here), happiness comes essentially from 'listening.' If one is too busy seeking happiness to listen, he or she will never find it.

"Listening" is literally the key, of course. One could not really tell God anything that God does not already know. Yet one must say something to start the conversation. The distinguished English author, C.S. Lewis, had something to say about the mystery of Gathering and the dilemma of the human being who must contact God in order to attain maturity, who has no knowledge of what to say, and is not perfectly sure he or she has heard God even after believing God has spoken. He wrote a poem called "Prayer":

>Master, they say that when I seem to be in speech with you,
>Since you make no replies, it's all a dream,
>One talker aping two.
>They are half right, but not as they imagine;
>Rather I seek in myself the things I meant to say,
>And, lo! the wells are dry.
>Then, seeing me empty, you forsake the listener's role,
>And through my dead lips breathe and into utterance wake
>The thoughts I never knew.
>And thus you neither need reply, nor can;
>Thus while we seem two talking, thou art One forever,

And I no dreamer, but thy dream.[37]

Even when you think no one has heard, you will begin to live the answer you did not think you received.

As noted above, beginning to love from a life of self-centeredness is sometimes very dramatic. Known as "Spiritual Transformation", or in the Scriptures, "conversion" (μετανοια), this progress sometimes causes an immediate and total change in life-style from selfishness to loving. Often visibly and even sensationally experienced in situations of extreme constraint, Alcoholics Anonymous meetings or contemplation sessions in jails, people return to being persons, or become loving persons right before one's eyes.[38] "Hopeless addiction" is an accepted medical diagnosis, even legally, and has almost no cure except through spiritual means. The regular recurrence of the miracle of the recovering A.A. person is the "laboratory proof" of the existence of spirituality and the transformation of persons embracing it. It is undeniable and can be viewed by anyone attending a few meetings.[39]

A major stumbling block to beginning a spirituality, as noted by the founders of Alcoholics Anonymous, is human pride. Pride, recognized by

---

[37] C.S. Lewis, "Prayer", from Poems, edited by Walter Hooper, Harcourt Brace Janovich, 1964. "Prayer", as one observer of human nature, William Inge, noted, "gives a man the opportunity of getting to know a gentleman he hardly ever meets. I don't mean his Maker, but himself."

[38] A Jesuit priest, who should know, has said that, when the history of the spirituality of the twentieth century is written, the most outstanding element in it will be the work of Alcoholics Anonymous. Anyone, like this author, who has seen persons literally go from the gutter and jail to a highly respected position in the human community, would readily agree. Cf., Monahan, Molly, Seeds of Grace: Reflections on the Spirituality of Alcoholics Anonymous. Riverhead Press: New York, 2001.

[39] "Spiritual Transformation" has sometimes been referred to as "Conversion." The latter term is not used here because it has sometimes been associated with turning to a religion and not necessarily turning to spirituality. Still, much knowledge about the process of such transformation can be gained from reading good discussions of "conversion." Two survey-type treatises can be readily recommended: Nock, A.D., Conversion: the Old and the New in Religion from Alexander the Great to Augustine of Hippo. Oxford University Press: London, 1933; Conn, Walter E., Conversion: Perspectives on Personal and Social Transformation. Alba House: New York, 1978.

the ancient Greeks as well as the great Christian mystics as the chief barrier to spirituality, takes many forms. Theologians divided sins into seven categories, the Seven Deadly Sins, and Pride was number one. The other six (Covetousness, Lust, Gluttony, Anger, Envy, and Sloth) were considered specific forms of Pride working itself into the various corners of human life.

A person overcome by drink needs only honestly to admit that they have lost control of their lives and humbly ask for help from the Higher Power. But this is easier said than done. "Honestly" and "Humbly" require a bit of squashing of the ego. "I can't handle this" and "I need outside Help" do not come readily to the mind of any of us.

Fear, say these experts, that I will not get what I really deserve or that others are getting what I deserve – in the form of drinking whatever they want and enjoying life – fear is the first expression of any and all forms of pride. Next comes self-delusion. Not only do people in the grips of some dysfunction lie to themselves about why they are dysfunctional, but they believe their own lies and act on them. Thirdly, self-seeking takes over and even family obligations are neglected in favor of drinking. Finally, self-pity takes over and drinking is done because "Everyone is always picking on me and I cannot understand why." So, the drinking of an alcoholic is pure selfishness – but wonderfully hidden under various pride-filled disguises. Alcoholics describe compulsive drinking as the highest form of selfishness short of murder, since the alcoholic only wants to consume more when even a drop is totally useless to him- or herself or anyone else.

Lest we think that we are in any way superior to the alcoholics, we note here that <u>everyone</u> has problems of pride. They are just not quite as noticeable as that of the alcoholic. In a way, the alcoholic is blessed with his malady of being allergic to alcohol. The rest of us may have problems that do not quickly destroy us, but lead us deeper and deeper into selfish lives where our use and abuse of others is subtle, but far reaching. If we are very talented, but simply greedy, we may end up causing deprivation, malnutrition, starvation and death to many others while sitting in a plush office in a high-rise, totally unaware of our horrible lives. Like carpet bombing from thirty thousand feet, we may have absolutely no idea of the innocent people we may be killing. Yet, we can hardly excuse ourselves by saying, "I had no knowledge of what was down there", or, "Yes, I suppose some collateral damage was inevitable." Simple observation of life around us and listening within to our deepest selves would easily have disabused us of making simplistic statements like these.

Motivation regularly plays a role in human decisions. Education provides options to aid in motivation. For the same reasons, love is made easier by knowing why one ought to love. A person that can love freely is the product of a prodigious effort by Order for almost 14 billion years. Recognition of this process may be a help to those struggling to overcome their failures and be especially enlightening to those who have given little thought to meaning.

ix. Spiritual Development
a. The Human Substrate

Research reveals that every human being is unique. Each has a peculiar set of talents. The process of becoming a loving person includes developing those talents so that they may be used in the service of love. Some persons' talents, like those of Mozart, are so startling as to be obvious to all and obviously benefit all. For most, however, our talents are not so obvious. To reach the goal set by the unfolding that brought "me" forth, "I" must develop the gifts I possess.

"Develop your giftedness," is easy to say. When a person does not know what his or her gifts are, a difficulty arises. A broadly based, "Liberal Arts" education for those so privileged will usually reveal the gifts, and then they can be cultivated. More often, a long life, slowly but surely arriving at clarity through benefiting from right decisions and learning from wrong ones, is the usual way to wisdom and understanding. The Order that seeks to produce loving persons appears to provide in every life the opportunities for choices that will lead to its fulfillment. That the mystery that brought us here from the Incomprehensible Explosion would merely dump us here and forget us does not seem either logical or probable based on the beautiful complexity of the smallest details found everywhere else.

Perhaps, the best advice for all us humans in this matter came from the late Joseph Campbell, author of the world-renowned work, "The Hero With A Thousand Faces."[40] He said that real joy accompanies the development of ones true giftedness, so "Follow your bliss!" In terms of the way we have been discussing this, "bliss" would be the "Voice of Order" inside everyone, giving them a sense of fulfillment, "bliss", each time they make progress towards becoming what they were designed to become.

This is true, of course, only for those of us who have enough resources to survive while making the effort. A world in which societies provided education for everyone until their "bliss" was attained would be a great leap forward for mankind. This usually means the government, since history so far shows us that education of the poor, the unfortunate, the unlucky, or especially the children of these same people, is usually neglected. Yet

---

[40] Campbell, Joseph, **The Hero With A Thousand Faces**. Princeton University Press, New Jersey, 1949.

discovering ones bliss seems to be very difficult for most without considerable education.

Perhaps here we might make a special note that these observations about governments providing free education might appear to be the result of a political position, but they are not. They come from the peculiar scattering of DNA and human history that shows that the location of talents cannot be predicted. They are based on the way that talents are scattered throughout the human species by Nature – talents needed for everyone.

The Incomprehensible Explosion seems merely to have produced the humans, caring little if anything for their political boundaries or philosophies. Humans, now provably a single family, obviously thrive when they share goods and talents with one another. When farmers developed the large, heavy ears of corn from the tiny spears of maize that they originally found, everyone benefited from the new abundance of food. To lock these methods of development in a safe as "Intellectual Property", with fees charged to anyone eating the larger ears, seems barbaric. This calls to mind those people who, in the 1840's, shipped out loads of foodstuffs grown in Ireland, where the Irish were starving, to England, where it was not needed, but made a profit.[41] Such people do not look like savages. They look just like other people. Our lack of spiritual development does not necessarily show on the outside.

A great danger, especially to the very talented, is to bask in his or her own uniqueness, earn a fortune from it, and do little or nothing for the human race. However, as far as anyone can determine, Order's interest is in every human being, and talents are scattered for the good of the community

---

[41] What is "legal" can, and often is, totally divorced from what is "right" or "good." Human beings, as noted especially and definitively in the famous Nuremberg Trials, are obliged to see the difference.

not just for the sake of the individual. "We" have evolved, not "you" or "me", and never a "you" or "me" apart from the "we." "All God's plans are family plans." Diametrically opposed to this way of thinking is what is known as "Rugged Individualism", itself a contradiction since everyone is a product of human cooperation.

This communal nature of evolution is not limited to people. Most higher animals survive and flourish because they live in herds or schools or other groups. Communal living provides a number of elements insuring existence. Humans are just far more complicated in their communities and in the possibilities of their development. Truly balanced adult humans are usually discovered to have been influenced by a whole range of persons in their communities. Though not always, the unbalanced or dysfunctional usually have a history of isolation and deprivation of socializing experiences, especially when accompanied beforehand by mental or emotional trauma. "It takes a village to raise a child" – "properly", of course.

Temptations always exist in any human life to reduce it to a commercial enterprise or to a pursuit of petty pleasures. To get an education so that one might get a job is a great denigration of the miracle of our being here on the Earth. Most universities, before they award a degree, insist that the students learn some history, philosophy and, perhaps, another language. This is to head off the mentioned temptation. Everyone decries the man who deserts his family to enjoy the pleasure of a new wife. He is despised because he is offending the meaning of his former family life. Similarly, someone who gets educated merely to earn money will probably die with a great deal of it, and with an unsuccessful life.

b. Spiritual Growth

The introduction of each of us in our uniqueness to an interpersonal relation with God, to a "Spirituality", varies almost as widely as the people who enter such a relation. This might be expected because any interpersonal relation between people is always nuanced by their personal histories, their education, and all the various "attitudes" that have been collected during their lives. When relating to God, a person might expect his or her uniqueness to affect that relationship as well. For clues to meaning one must not merely examine life, but ones particular life.

The dramatic motion of jump-starting spiritual development, mentioned in the instance of alcoholics and convicts above, is not the ordinary way of transformation. Although punctuated often by a "conscious moment", the usual growth in becoming a person is in gradual, almost imperceptible steps during the most ordinary circumstances of very ordinary lives. For example, I hate to be disturbed when I read the paper in the morning, but I am continually bombarded by children seeking my attention. One day, listening to some prompting within, I decide that the children are more important than the paper and I give up my paper for a few years. I have made a step in the direction of maturity. Similarly, I stop for a beer on the way home from work. I waste time that is needed at home and money that is needed at home. One day, under an "impulse", I decide to go straight home. I take a step to maturity. Love is a kind of dying to self but, like seeds buried in the earth, in dying to selfishness the human flowers. After a thousand steps, a wise and loving human person changes everyone they encounter with their love.

Most persons have been loved as children and know what love is. Progressing from being loved to becoming a loving person, as noted above, is not automatic. The process of most humans appears to be halting and filled with compromises as we struggle to overcome our instinctive self-centeredness and grow into persons. Temptation to rationalization is, apparently, fairly constant. "I am developed enough in my concern for others and now it's time to look out for Number One," is heard often in some form or other. Followed as advice, it distorts the maturation process.[42]

What is obvious is that one can have the most beautiful, well-toned body in the world, the most money, property, or wives or lovers in the world, be the best shot at marksmanship, the best fisherman at fishing or the most skillful at any art and, if one has not also developed love, putting others and their needs ahead of the self when the situation demands it, one is a failure as a human being. The basic rule of life is that I must move the human race forward in love – because that is the direction visible in the unfolding so far – and not spread my toxicity, my selfishness, among my fellow humans.

Conversely, one can live the most marginal existence in rags, be despised and beaten by those among whom one stays, and still be the "best" person there. That rather unkempt, dark-skinned, ill-smelling person, cousin, working in my yard or digging the trenches for my new sauna, may be better at unselfish love than I am and, as a result, is a better human being than I am. If he listens to the Someone within him, he may be far ahead of me spiritually.

---

[42] "The main battlefield for good is not the open ground of the public arena but the small clearing of each heart. Meanwhile, the lot of widows and homeless children is very hard, and it is to their defense, not God's, that the self-righteous should rush." Martel, Vann, Life of Pi. Harcourt, Inc.: London, 2001, chap.25.

A poem wherein a nineteenth century British soldier celebrates this fact has become famous. The soldier is provided water by an Indian servant who goes about his duties with meticulous care, great bravery, and personal grace. The servant is killed ("…a bullet came an' drilled the beggar clean") just after rescuing his overlord by dragging him to safety and giving him a drink of water. His dying words were, "I hope that you enjoyed your drink of water." The soldier speaks to the dead servant:

> "Though I've belted you and flayed you,
>   By the living God that made you,
>   You're a better man than I am, Gunga Din."[43]

With confidence in access to the Source of our unfolding, that is, by having a developed spirituality, we are always, no matter what our circumstances, able to develop into loving beings.

Even as a child, maybe of six or seven years, the mystery of life envelops the would-be lover. Walking down the aisle between the desks, a classmate drops a pencil. Seeing it fall, the child, usually based on what happens in its home, stoops down and hands the classmate their dropped pencil. The person begins to form. Another might say, "You dropped your pencil" and a different result begins to happen. A third might laugh. A fourth might kick the pencil farther from the one dropping it. As long as the child is to some extent making its own decision, its very soul is being formed and its ultimate destiny being prepared.

One obvious part of loving that must be stressed is forgiveness. Children are very good at it. The ones who kicked the pencil farther away or the ones who laughed at its dropping are often found playing with the one they abused the very next day. Refusing to react negatively to a wide variety of

---

[43] Rudyard Kipling, "Gunga Din".

hurts and then to forget them completely seem to be part of loving. The more one forgives and forgets, the easier the practice becomes, and the more mature the loving person appears.

A great lesson can be learned here from ancient philosophers, a lesson later Christianized and made a central part of traditional Christianity. It is that good choices are greatly aided by self-discipline. Fasting from food, especially food one does not need for basic nutrition, strengthens the will to make the decisions to love. Practice of self-denial makes the decision, to put the other ahead of the self, easier. Classically etched upon Western History, the Christian practice of "Lent" was, and is, a period of self-mortification, a preparation for one making the decision to be baptized, that is, to go under the water and die to ones selfish interests. Maturity is in large part the delay of self-gratification. To love anyone when they need loving, all the way from feeding the hungry to burying the dead, is made easy by practice, and ease in doing the loving thing when it is needed is called "virtue."[44]

The progress of spiritual development is usually visible in the lives of the persons progressing. Love, peace, joy, kindness, and so on, are the natural fruits of a spiritually centered life according to some of the greatest philosphers. If the result of ones "prayers" is war, destruction, sadness, hatred, and so on, one knows that one has made a wrong turn somewhere. Most spiritual journeys require checking various decisions out with other persons who know they are on a journey. However, before any truly visible progress is made, people must overcome all of the traumas and dysfunctional lessons bestowed upon them by their parents, their culture, and their own misadventures. Persons with deeply dysfunctional

---

[44] Aritotle (384-322 BCE), known as The Philosopher, noted, "True happiness flows from the possession of wisdom and virtue, and not from the possession of external goods."

backgrounds may, after a life-time, appear to have as their only success that they do not drink the alcoholic beverages for which they have a fatal allergy. Depending upon what hill they had to climb to overcome their alcoholism, this success may be a more heroic life lived than that of Mother Theresa. Since no one knows the demons that other might have to face, or have already faced in their life, making judgments about the spiritual progress of another human being without knowing a great deal about them personally and in detail is absolutely futile and totally misguided.[45]

In the quest of going from a simple beginning to a maturely developed spirituality, most of us live our lives somewhere in the middle between serial killer with none and Mother Theresa. Some are lives of "quiet desperation" looking for meaning. Most love is sidetracked at the moment of decision by "the cares and pleasures of life." We fail because we do not see the battle within ourselves in which we are engaged. Although destined to be magnificent lovers and heroes, we are too often willing to settle for a small piece of its promise. To place what is best for the Other ahead of ourselves when we <u>cannot</u> see that we are being challenged by the very meaning of life itself, is the essence of love. True love does not really ask "why?" or "for whom?" True love just goes ahead and gives what it can.

The precise difference between a person who loves and one who loves greatly is the ability to love without seeing where love leads, trusting in God completely. We apparently are designed to be "cared for" and, if we reject "listening", we proceed at our own peril. We are free, of course. But we must stop and ask that peculiar question that every person has inside them, "Why was I born to these parents, in this time and place, with these talents,

---

[45] Regarding the behavior of others, one might legitimately say, "I wouldn't do that." What one may never say is, "That person is bad", implying that one knows how God feels about that person.

and under these world conditions?" A totally dominating Order is found in the smallest bits of the Universe. That this same Order would not wish to exert its influence in the latest complexities, the humans, does not really make sense. A person with a developed spirituality will pray, that is, ask the Someone every day, "What am I to do now?"

When enough loving souls are formed, the very culture of a society becomes impregnated with the loving message of life. Human life itself is moved to greater gathering and centering and its future becomes more stable, and open to greater possibilities. Love turns out to be the practical answer to all of human striving. What principles of loving action are incorporated into the fiber of a society are the true gifts that are passed on to the next generation. For a generation to be spontaneously kind and generous, to be caring and concerned about the others around them because that is all they experience as they mature – that is to become truly civilized.

x. Meaning

The more we go into the paeleological and cosmological depths of our world and the more we penetrate the cosmic depths of origins, the more orderly everything appears. Almost no chaos or disorder exists and some of the most important building blocks of the Universe come to be in the violence of cosmic fires and explosions. This Order could <u>never</u> be called chance. It is so incredibly nuanced in the case of some living things with truly bizarre forms, like Sea Horses, or some activities, like those of Archer Fish that knock their food out of bushes with 'shots' of water, even the most objective person feels the Order. They feel thrust into the Presence of intelligence and power beyond all imagination – perhaps a "Someone." This phenomenal Order is one of the reasons why people, in general, like to visit natural wonders or wilderness parks. Shorn of the inroads of man, both in their beauty and their sublimity they exude the Presence from whence they came.

This is the condition of Things that caused Albert Einstein to make that remark that the odds of our world happening by chance are about the same as an unabridged dictionary resulting from an explosion in a print shop. If not by chance, then by an Order so far reaching that it is immediate to the existence of everything that is. That is to say, "chance" is <u>not involved.</u> Some place for chance might exist within the larger confines of a planned order. To deny this is to swallow such a chain of coincidences that we simply would not have come to be here from the Incomprehensible Explosion. But we are here. Volcanoes erupting may appear to erupt willy-nilly, but if they do not erupt, the spheres are not properly formed to bring forth living things. If "accident" is anywhere involved in the system, then we are back to the impossible production of the unabridged dictionary.

To deny the larger embrace of Order is to return to absurdity. Moreover, because <u>persons</u> are some of the things produced by this immense interaction of spheres – a fact quite beyond the sheer number and complexity of the zones needed for the other life forms – Order must contain, in the same form or a higher one, all the attributes of "Person." Even the fact that random chance is involved in the progress of evolution is not by that fact a proof that Order does not hold chance in its sway. When the inevitable result of the collusion of chance, vast numbers, and time, is progress of a describable nature, gathering, complicating, and centering, one must conclude that chance itself is in the grasp of Law. When something occurs by orderly design, and not by chance, it is called "meaning-full." The Universe is "meaning-full."

A reluctance to acknowledge Meaning and its Author, God, arises from a sense of insecurity left over from ancient times. Some humans still attribute "divine" or "supernatural" qualities to things they do not understand. As scientists made real inroads into the mystery of things, direct attribution of mysteries to the gods was debunked.

Too often, the scientists projected their results into the future and decided that in a matter of time, they would dispel all mysteries. They would rid the world of all "divine" and "supernatural" notions since the latter were all superstitions. As noted, the few centuries of solving nature's mysteries have resulted only in more questions and more mystery, not less. While hardly any humans are left who attribute to "the gods" the things that they do not understand, neither are any left, scientists included, who think we have done any more than scratch the surface of the mystery of life. If anything, science has brought us closer to facing God and Meaning.

Still lingering fears of acknowledging "Someone-unfolding-a-Universe" are understandable on two counts, both coming from the history of humanity. On the one hand, in the early history of mankind persons claiming to know who God was, and what God wanted people to do, produced absolute misery for immense numbers of persons, and sometimes whole societies. On the other, the more people realize Someone is there, the more some of them seem unable to resist making claims of extraordinary knowledge of God. They do this because they think they actually do know the wishes of God, or they do not believe in God at all and are merely taking advantage of the people who do. Yet, to ignore the Presence of the Someone because a mere fellow-mortal might make phony claims, however eloquent, is folly. In the long run, we probably need not worry very much about phony claims.

From one point of view, Humanity might <u>need</u> to recognize God for its own good, and even its own proper development. The Someone appears to have so arranged our unfolding that, when the blind laws of Gathering and the directions of instinct come to an end in a free, conscious being, the next directions for life are hidden in a freely developed relationship with God. The notion of this relating-to-Someone is universal.

> "My brother kneels (so saith Kabir)
> To stone and brass in heathen-wise,
> But in my Brother's voice I hear
> My own unanswered agonies.
> His God is as his Fates assign –
> His prayer is all the world's – and mine."[46]

Meaning for the Human Race, then, is to be found, finally, in habitually performing those highest actions known to the species, deeds of selfless love, and in relating to the Maker for guidance. The evidence in the process of the unfolding of humanity culminates in the Seeker finding the Universe producing human beings with conscious knowledge, and with many informed activities and decisions that reach a zenith in love. This is evident from what makes humans grow, mature, and become great.

Anyone claiming to know the Orderer and failing to talk about love, including forgiveness and self-sacrifice is, *ipso facto*, ignorant. Anyone claiming secret knowledge from God is probably lying or self-deceived. Anyone contradicting the known facts and processes of the Universe has some private agenda that will eventually fail the one who follows it. God would have to be the Author of the content of Science and, thus, no possible

---

[46] From the writings attributed to Kabir, a man of 15th Century India, held to be a saint by both Moslems and Hindus. Cited by Rudyard Kipling in, <u>Kim</u>, leading off Chapter XIV.

conflict ought exist between science and what is said about the Someone.[47] Anyone using fear to push an agenda is suspect. Any Universe which unfolds for 13.7 billion years, always getting more centered and complicated, and finally reaching its highest plane in the form of unselfish love, is not one in which the Orderer is to be feared – unless one is partial to abuse, hatred, and doing harm.

We have strayed into areas usually reserved to members of a religion. But they, too, must not violate the axioms of history. Persons following ancient Sacred Books to find directions to God, the Way to Live, or the Meaning of Life, must read those words in the context of the time they were written and in light of the knowledge of the world known at that time. Regard must be held for the fact that old sacred books are read in translations, a process easily open to error. In an even wider sense, a Seeker (which we all are, in some way) must be wary of anything sacred conveyed through the frailty of human nature. The Seeker should listen to persons of demonstrable authority about such matters, and preferably to authorities with ancient credentials, knowledge of ancient languages, and long-collected wisdom.

"A God who makes a creature totally unable to achieve the purpose of its existence" is an oxymoron. However, since the Universe is vast beyond comprehension, and the creatures in it diverse beyond comprehension, wide latitude must be given to ideas about the meaning of existence or any existent. We do not know clearly or certainly what God is doing. When we see tragedy and cataclysm, we do not know what is really happening. We are reasoning creatures, but still mere creatures. Love came from the Incomprehensible Explosion. Love will undoubtedly prevail in the ultimate

---

[47] St. Thomas Aquinas, in the 13th Century, said, "Creation is God's first revelation."

unfolding of the cosmic process. We can, and indeed we must, examine life and our lives, but we must never try to second-guess the Someone.[48]

Faith, and even religion, may ultimately be necessary for the average human to live a good and loving life. That is not in dispute. What we say here is a product of a reasonable Seeker, and is prior to, and a part of, any faith: Someone did the Big Bang and the Whole of it is going somewhere very deliberately. More will be said on Faith within the treatment of Christianity later in this treatise.

xi. Death and Life

We do know of one problem that nothing will ever eliminate, and that is, we all <u>die</u>. But could it be that we humans, even dying, are not "There" yet? Could we be going Somewhere Else? Through death? Is there an "…undiscovered country from whose bourn no traveler returns"?[49] The basic Law of All Things continues to rule. The more gathered, complex, and centered the Thing, the more conscious it is. From the Incomprehensible Explosion a direction emerges, going from Particles to Things to Life to Thought.

Though Living Things die, overall movement towards complexity and interiority might continue. Many think dead humans live on, and some think animals do, too. The fact that life after death has been often elaborated is evidence of this possibility, and Going Somewhere Else finds more support. This is not idle speculation. They tap into a "Logic of Unfolding" that finds a base in billions of years of Order going in a discernible direction.

---

[48] People who say, "My Mother died of cancer so God does not exist", or "The Nazi Holocaust proves God does not exist" are such persons. We simply must not play God – things are too complicated.
[49] Shakespeare, <u>Hamlet</u>, III, 1.

Surviving death is, of course, not demonstrable in the sense of the Natural Sciences' "proof", but is demonstrable and predictable from the evidence of the unfolding. Some items are known by presence of their effects, some by the presence of their causes. Some can be verified by controlled experiments, some cannot. We were <u>absolutely</u> sure another side of the moon existed before we went and looked. (This is not to say that you cannot find anyone who would say, "No other side of the moon exists.")

Entropy is a universal law of the Cosmos. It says that everything that is done in the universe takes energy. Noting that, however vast, a finite amount of energy exists, the same law says that some time in the future nothing will exist. We will simply run out of energy, "dark matter" and "dark energy" not withstanding. Just as we die, so, too, will the Cosmos. We will return to that vast, dark, and empty place of Nothing-At-All. Some scientists conjecture we will be one large Black Hole, sometimes described as "The Big Crunch."[50]

Or will we? One of the strange effects of the activities of reflective self-awareness and love is that they seem to defy the law of entropy. As one great scientist, Pierre Teilhard de Chardin, noted, we go as far as any animal after being fed a slice of bread, but, in addition to the going, we have so many <u>ideas</u> as well – far too many to be explained by the bit of food. The life of the abstract idea seems to ignore the limitations of matter. Moreover, when we reflect, when we know that we know, and know that we are knowing at the same time, we defy matter. We, as it were, are able to touch the tip of our finger with the tip of the same finger! Having arrived at the pinnacle of the evolution of the Cosmos, the <u>person</u> of man seems to slip right out of it into a thought-world.

---

[50] Cf. Magueijo, <u>Faster...</u>, p.66.

Mankind is said to live in three dimensions but some quite reputable thinkers have added Time as a fourth dimension, and suggested others.[51] Humans carry on a life that is certainly not one of the first four dimensions. They boldly, if not presumptuously, say things like, "Let the Universe equal X", or patently irrational but very useful things like, "*i equals the square root of minus 1*." Perhaps human life could survive the dying of the material world.

The same Pierre Teilhard de Chardin, a Jesuit Priest as well as a paleontologist – and one of the discoverers of Peking Man -- observed that the patterns of unfolding are visible throughout the Universe. Moreover, they are consistent through eons of time and indicate a couple of new possible levels to help answer the "Where to?" question.[52] All living things, he noted, become more complex and centered, but do so by gathering with the world around them. Where, he asked, would thoughtful, self-reflective, loving persons go?

Wherever they went, the direction would be more internally centered, more complex, but gathered with the other persons around them. Therefore, the natural prolepsis of the present condition of human beings – if they love – would be a kind of joining of minds with one another in that immaterial dimension spoken of above as the realm of ideas. Teilhard called this new place of being the "Noosphere" – the "Sphere of Mind" (from the Greek, "νους", "mind").

This new sphere is another biosphere in that it has life, is a world of thought-beings at least – and maybe more – where persons gather. Also,

---

[51] Ibid., pp.34-35, 144.
[52] The foundational ideas for much of the thought around the unfolding universe are to be found in two works of Teilhard de Chardin, The Phenomenon of Man, Perennial Library, Harper and Row, 1959, and The Divine Milieu, Perennial Library, Harper and Row, 1959.

though keeping each their individuality, they are in union with all the other persons "there." Or, perhaps this new sphere is populated by all those who do love, and the ones that do not love simply cannot move to "there" after here. Perhaps one arrives at the next life precisely because one has loved, or loved enough. Perhaps one does not need to do anything but die to find oneself in another world.

For Teilhard, the complexities of the elements of the Big Bang, gathered into humans after the appropriate billions of years, seem to have been able to form what traditional religion calls an "immortal soul." This part of the human, formed by his or her life experiences, is formed of, and lives without the regular matter of our five senses. This living thing would not, in the understanding of modern science, need to be a special creation of God as some theologies claim. It could be a composit of elements, of Dark Matter and Dark Energy, scattered in the original, Incomprehensible Explosion by the very Word of God which the same theologies say was involved in "everything that was made." We will look at this again when we look at Christianity.

This new, "next" world might, like the present world to someone who observed the Incomprehensible Explosion, have all kinds of dimensions which escape our ability to imagine. However, the bare outline of this world would be quite similar to the world of the first complex living things that were formed by the gathering of many simple things into a single living complexity. The Laws of Order are found everywhere consistent in the Universe and, since we have come to be through these processes, where we are headed ought not be an exception. Whoever could have predicted, seeing the Incomprehensible Explosion, that living things, like frogs or roses, would come from its seemingly chaotic violence? And, seeing it, whoever would have dreamed of poets and lovers? The hand of Order is full of surprises.[53]

With a God who is incomprehensibly beautiful and loving, the Source of all beauty and love, we might expect that the natural next step of humans would be a "place" where persons who love would be together. This "place" would fit not only the Laws of increased complexity and centering, but would also satisfy the poetic projections of human aspirations for ultimate meaning and ultimate justice. For obvious reasons, humans have from their inception speculated about a life after this one and about a realm of the dead. However inaccurate or "primitive" their "hunch" is, that some such realm exists is borne out by science in the pattern of its Laws. This is not just a happy coincidence. This is a result argued from evidence. This is Einstein saying to the theorists about the atom, "It might be a theory, but stand way back." God, the Author of Love, now has brought forth beings capable of sharing love with God. Perhaps God is available in the Noosphere or some "place" just beyond.

Perhaps the poets are correct. They have written about this often. William Wadsworth Longfellow said in his, <u>Psalm of Life</u>:

> "Tell me not, in mournful numbers, Life is but an empty dream
> and the soul is dead that slumbers, and things are not what they seem.
> Life is real! Life is earnest! And the grave is not its goal;
> 'Dust thou art, to dust returnest' was not spoken of the soul."

In addition to the poets, common wisdom has always pointed to a greater meaning to life for humans than simply living and dying. A newspaper

---

[53] We must acknowledge in passing that the philosopher, Aristotle, in the 4th Century B.C.E., opined that a number of beings called "Separated Substances", intellectual beings without bodies who moved the celestial spheres, had to exist. They fit neatly, he thought, into the niche between humans, who had bodies but also an intellectual life, and the perfect, spiritual Leader of the Universe, "Who," as he said, "is One."

advice columnist, trying to deal with a letter from a reader complaining of a dread of funerals, wrote:

> "...it is no exaggeration to say that they [funerals] are a defining element of civilization. We wouldn't think much of a society, no matter what its other achievements, that threw its deceased into a disposal like garbage. Funerals honor the dead, comfort the bereaved and give life a sense of meaning and continuity." ("Miss Manners", San Francisco Chronicle, 5/14/03)

The great Roman orator and sage, Cicero, felt that life after death was a part of the thinking of every person. He backed up his self-assurance on the matter when he noted, "Without the hope of immortality, no one would be willing to die for their country."

Perhaps Love is as far as we can go towards the "Why?" of things, and we do not get much further with the "Where to?" of things. Starting with an orderly explosion, the universe progressed through galaxies, solar systems, worlds with living things, then to sensible and rational beings to loving persons. No special intervention by the Orderer (or Presence or Someone) appears to be necessary in the evolution of these loving persons. We might conclude, since the final product so far seems to be selfless, loving persons, that the original motive for the Order was selfless, maybe even selfless love. The "Why?" answer would then lie in the area of "giving" or "sharing" life and love since the Orderer implicitly had to have self-reflective awareness and love. This factor points to a "There" beyond the here and now. Maybe the "Why?" is answered by a sharing of love between the Orderer and the Orderer's creation.

Considering that "uniting" ("Gathering") is one of the basic operations of the Universe after the scattering of the initial explosion, the ultimate uniting of the Cause of the explosion with the now-intelligent, personable product of the explosion, humans, would be a perfectly logical extension. The scattering particles from the Incomprehensible Explosion are slowly gathered into elements and energies. The elements and energies are gathered into things. The things are gathered into ever more complex things, until living things, sensing things and knowing things are present in at least one complex world with a Biosphere. These latest living things, now resembling the Originator in many ways, are gathered by love into more or less successful societies of more or less loving persons, but all the while dying off individually. All the loving persons regret seeing their loved ones die, and generate ideas of ritual burial and "places" in an after-life. Without explicit reference to the scientific laws of Gathering, persons from every corner of the Earth look to a new life of gathering with their loved ones. Why? Because Gathering is such a fundamental condition of human being that it forms naturally in the human mind as a probable explanation of the conundrum of dying.

When these logical inferences from the Laws of Gathering are put along side the need for justice in cases of the torture and death of the innocent (such as the Nazi holocaust), and the existence of Beauty and Sublimity in the world, life after death becomes not only probable, but most likely. When they are laid along side the logically necessary existence of Someone (Whom we call God), these same inferences are as near to certainty as anything gets in this world, easily surpassing the evidence for the certainty of the atom and the twisted evidence that the whole is meaningless.

What we have discovered about the "Where?" and "Why?" of humankind puts us at the center of a most interesting mystery, and a life that rivals the adventures of Tolkein's Middle Earth. We arrive without our consent amid people we did not choose, of a sex and race we had nothing to say about. Wherever we arrive, we are challenged to learn to love, and to create love all around us. We are challenged by every day we live, and we do not know how many that will add up to. Unlike the drama that we wondered about above, life turns out not to be a play at all, but a serious reality, sometimes where people die horribly by the thousands. People's choices – our own choices – are of tremendous significance to ourselves and others.

To anyone familiar with what has been said about the unfolding universe and its condition of being fraught with direction and meaning, those not living lives with a sense of adventure and purpose appear passing strange. To many academics, people who spend their lives trying to acquire money look very odd. On the other hand, people chasing money think that those who, say, spend their lives looking through microscopes or translating obscure treatises, look equally odd. The money-chasers are always wanting to know what kind of higher income or increased financial advantage taking this or that course will bring. If none is immediately apparent, they sneer at it. People who withdraw into a tidy world of seeking only to increase the comforts of daily existence look quite odd to the dedicated teacher and the graduate philosophy student – and vice versa!

People who think that the everyday decisions of life are of little or no significance appear to denigrate this great and mysterious gift of life to those aware of the evidence for meaning. Apart from those whom human folly has relegated to a struggling, subsistence living, the world seems to be roughly divided into three kinds, those who pursue life with meaning, those who do not, and those seeking meaning. To capture the actual feeling of meaninglessness, one need only walk into an adult disco or seedy bar on

Saturday night, as this author did often in his misspent youth. It is overwhelmingly depressing.

Almost fourteen billion years in the making, the human is faced with the task of becoming a free agent choosing good, love, over evil, selfishness. The effort of each choice changes the self, putting it further on the road to unity with others in a loving community, or to the prison of the self where ones blighted ego is ones only final companion. The immortal selves, constructed out of the same ethereal decisions of loving and hating for a various numbers of years, survive the entropy of the Incomprehensible Explosion. We arrive to the place for which we were destined at our making, but also in a state made by ourselves.

But such ideas are not in favor with most now in charge of the world. The present state of the Earth is one in which the majority of people of power do not share the vision of the Earth as a place of a single family of humans drawn by their Orderer to become persons who love one another. Seduced by greed, vested self-interest, lust for power, or superficial differences between the appearance of different humans, like skin color or a preferred way of viewing the Someone, people seem bent at least on denying their familial relationship with others, and at worst on eliminating them. Unless all humans realize not only their relationship to all others, but their need for the others' talents and help in their own development, we will never get to a state of loving easily and spontaneously, a place where all obviously are being enticed. The measure of the progress of a nation is the extent to which it cares for the most vulnerable of its citizens. One measure of the progress of the world would certainly be the cessation of that most foolish of human inventions, war.

But the observations about the "Where to?" of humans after their years of this earthly life, however reasonable, have a more speculative quality about them than what may be said about our coming to be here and what our development as persons consists of in the here and now. We have reached one end of our quest. What the universe is all about during this life is, and will be, the formation of persons, beings that can think, develop their talents, and love. If the universe is about more than that, if it is about the combined effort of the laws of Order and the free cooperation of human persons, it must await the gathering, complicating and centering of persons who are also free not to do that. If we are to progress beyond where we are, laws curbing greed, war, prejudice, and all human behavior that directly or indirectly forces upon others its private notion of where this great Mystery is going, would seem to be one solution. However, that is probably not the way, considering failures of the past. More probably, education that places history, philosophy, anthropology – in general, ideas and ideals – as the best things one can study to prepare for life, will be eliminated in favor of those that help in "getting a job."

In the final analysis, perhaps more reasons exist for love finally prevailing. Perhaps there is more evidence for optimism. Something clearly upbeat can be heard in a few more lines from the poet, Longfellow, quoted above:

> "Lives of great men all remind us we can make our lives sublime,
> And, departing, leave behind us footprints on the sands of time….
> Let us, then, be up and doing, with a heart for any fate;
> Still achieving, still pursuing, Learn to labor and to wait."

xiv. Conclusion

The scientific answer to the basic question of life, "What is it all about?" can be found in the Universe by examining its direction and the laws that direct it. In this our corner of the universe, a direct line unfolds in the Cosmos from the first explosion, initiating its movement, to the present. That line, governed by universal laws of gathering together, arranging, and rearranging the stuff of the original explosion, has gone from simple conglomerates to simple things to complex things, to living things, to knowing things, and then to present-day persons and their unique ability to love. The laws involved are three-fold in kind, Gathering, Complicating, and Centering, all permeated with an over-arching Order making them consistent throughout Time and Space. They appear to be very complex laws, but each scientific advance seems to indicate an ultimate simplicity and uniformity. The arrangements of the Things produced, from the simplest particles or waves of light, have moved from simple association to atoms to molecules to complex molecules to mega-molecules to living things. The living things have moved from one-celled animals with simple nuclei to all kinds of different families and species. The "higher" animals have moved from simpler functions with nerve centers to human beings with highly developed brains. The psychic life of these same animals has moved from sluggish awareness of the immediate world around it, through feeling, sensing at a distance, to conscious life.

Conscious life is quite different from Knowledge and Thinking Life. A special moment – a leap into a very different form – separates being conscious from thinking. A thinking being might be aware, for example, like a cat is aware of a mouse. We say the cat "knows" the mouse is there.

We might even extend this to the great apes who even "know" when they have lied. However, to ruminate about "apes" and "cats" in general, to have an "idea" of "cat" and form a definition of "cat" with a whole zoological sub-science connected to it, is quite another matter. It is "knowing" far beyond "to be thinking" and far beyond the association of a few ideas. The great ape may even develop so far as to lie for its own ends, but does it know that it has harmed another, or maybe even itself by its lie? Not so that experiments have been able to tell.

This new complication of humans is achieved when knowing moves from crude and simple awareness of the world to abstract thought and to reflective self-awareness that knows and, simultaneously, knows that it knows. All the evidence indicates that this evolution is in one direction of complexity, and the more highly complex specimens never come before the less complex ones have already made their appearance.

The appearance of reflective self–awareness created a totally new situation for the whole Cosmos. For the first time a Thing made by the Laws of Order could choose to engage its own self into the procession of the Universe. To take an extreme case, if all of the atomic bombs now made were to be detonated tomorrow, within a very short time all of life on Earth would be poisoned. The unfolding of the Earth story would be definitively interrupted, if not totally ended, by the very ones the Universe produced!

The development of conscious beings to becoming complicated social beings, living in nation states and erecting institutes of higher learning to produce artists, scientists and sages, has come about slowly, over thousands of years. Consciousness, itself, seems to have developed in human beings through five stages: the Magical, the Mythical, the Perceptival, the Integral, and the Self-operative. At the Self-operative, "Listening to Order", a kind of consciousness of ones entire environment, seems to characterize the stage.

Sometimes the laws of Order governing this unfolding have seemed paradoxical. Basic animal instincts for competition and dominance played a vital role in the ascent of early bipeds to human beings. Gaining the faculty of free choice, for example, appears to have come out of the multiple alternatives gradually assimilated from efforts to overcome other competitors and other dominators within our species. But the final product, appearing only in the last few thousand years, appears contrary to competition and dominance. For love to triumph, basic instincts have to be suppressed, at least in most circumstances.

Finally, then, the complication of Love has come upon the scene, transforming even abstract and scientific knowledge. A really new thing, probably the most neglected aspect in the literature about Evolution, love is far more representative of Gathering, Complicating, and Centering than any phenomenon prior to its appearance. It has the possibility of making all the difference in the story of mankind.

Love, the leap beyond reflex self-awareness to reflective self-awareness and the simple association with other human beings, has its own way of complicating as might be expected in a universally Gathering and Complicating Universe. This complexity is called "Personification." A human can be as dull as an ant, although feeling and thinking, but go through life like any Primate, albeit a very complicated one. A human, even with reflective self-awareness, can go through life trying solely to improve his position in the tribe, using whatever means are available. All such behavior has been carefully outlined in Primatology by contemporary anthropologists.[54] The behavior is highly complex, perhaps symbolized by the evidence that chimpanzees have died of grief.

However, when a human is loved selflessly, a strange transformation takes place. A being that was merely gathering with its fellow-humans for food, clothing and shelter, and trying to establish dominance in his or her tribe, now becomes a force for the education, development and concerned care of other humans. These factors make the other humans in contact with them more capable of Gathering and Complicating, pushing the evolutionary force (the orthogenetic character), the Order within us, towards the next, unknown phase.

In view of what has been said about primitive instinct and gradual evolution, the most important thing about this whole Search is that we are yet in the middle of it! Rich and powerful persons, acting out their primitive instincts of competition and dominance, still become predators upon their own brothers and sisters! They do not suppress the instincts with which they are born, but which are now destructive of humankind. Instead, they hone them sharply and, viewing others as objects instead of cousins, they abuse them for the sake of gaining power and/or wealth. With their power they even tout the competition as highly beneficial, all the while making sure the playing field is not level. However kind privately, they fail even to approach love in their "public" lives.[55]

---

[54] For understanding the insights of contemporary Anthropology into Primatology, cf., Frans de Waal, Chimpanzee Politics: Power and Sex Among the Apes. The Johns Hopkins University Press: Baltimore, 1982. For a broadened, complimentary view by a psychiatrist, cf., Arnold M. Ludwig, King of the Mountain: The Nature of Political Leadership. The University Press of Kentucky: Lexington, 2002.

[55] These same "leaders" do not, as far as this author can tell, know what they are doing. They seem to speak out of a sense of entitlement, as if to say, "The reason I have so much is because I am more worthy." This is especially noticeable when sensible inheritance taxes are put in place. They are attacked by the recipients as if the next generation, in spite of getting a head start by being given every human advantage from wealthy and powerful parents, earned all the money their parents had left. Most Countries, using law

Love is a matter of the free choice of each person. Therefore, the pervasiveness of love in the world is determined by persons of a single species, and not by the instinct or the inherent Order of the unfolding Cosmos, as hitherto has been the case. If through love, then, we are to proceed to the next phase of the cosmos, then the next phase is significantly in our hands, and not simply achieved by force of Law and the dynamic energy of the first explosion.

A "next phase" beyond death seems not only possible, but an entirely probable outcome, considering the stages of unfolding that humankind has passed through to get to this phase. From the most primitive gathering of the simplest gravitational pull to the union of two persons deeply in love, the Process has an inner logic to it that both reveals the Orderer from whence gathering comes, and suggests a gathering with each other <u>and</u> the Orderer that is most compelling. To immerse oneself in the meaningfulness and direction that appears in every natural phenomenon as well as in the orderly mass movement of the Cosmos, is to feel intensely the need and certitude of the "next phase." To define "knowledge" so that cosmic direction is not included, or that poetry is considered a waste of time and that life must ultimately be nonsense, is to fail to take account of the cosmic process by which humanity expresses its fullness. That the whole of life would be nonsense while every minute process and part that brought about the whole are filled with designed, progressive structure is patently absurd.

The final answer to the question of meaning turns out to be "whatever we make it"! What it <u>might</u> mean, and apparently <u>should</u> mean, is Love, the

---

to promote the general welfare, say to them, "Money and property are power. You can only keep so much of them or, through the power they give you, you might take it all, or not leave enough for others."

sharing of life and its joys with others, both for the sake of our mutual joy and for the sake of achieving joy beyond this life. This joy is the clear objective of the fourteen billion year process producing us, and the direction of the Order within us.

When activated by Love, people come together in peace, thrive, share food, shelter, clothing, and knowledge. Especially notable in close-knit families, they help to develop and to share the unique talents that are found in each and every human member. This cooperative effort makes everyone's life better. We have no idea what great things could come from our making everyone's life better because the few times we have tried, we have been greatly distracted by those among us who seem never to tire of commerce for the sake of commerce and not just to improve life.

To them, a human being is a "Consumer" of their products, not a person. This is true even when they have more than enough to live a life of luxury. When they begin to have so much that others cannot get enough, they often erect strong police forces and armies to protect the too-much they already have. Some seem to want strife when peace is what makes everyone thrive. When they find out how much money can be made selling armament, they foster war. In our analysis, they have succumbed to the temptation of Greed, a by-product of the primitive competition to survive gone amok. They sometimes do this in the name of "Freedom" but freedom is not license. The freedom to be greedy is like the freedom to shout "Fire!" in a crowded theater when no fire exists. This "freedom" does not exist, even if the laws of a nation would say it does.

The key to the future may be in the development of a new individual Spirituality. The children of Order, humans, largely create the world they live in by following the life that they decide upon. If most are barbarians, life will be mostly barbaric. The decisions we make come from the world we live in and from the Order we grasp and make active in our lives. We are quite free to do whatever pleases us or do what helps everyone. We have a strong tendency to the former, but a nagging suspicion, coming from the Order in and around us, that we ought to do the latter. To do the latter we need consciously to "listen" to Order – to develop a Spirituality. To develop a Spirituality, with the slender evidence we have from religions and such movements as Alcoholics Anonymous, requires a humble request of the Orderer that our life be directed by that Someone. Many find this difficult. The author hopes these pages make it easier.

Peace on Earth, the product of most of the people listening to Order, however difficult to obtain, is in our hands. The future is in our hands.

II. Jesus of Nazareth

> ""It was necessary for human beings to be instructed by a divine Revelation because only a few people, after a long time, and with a great many errors mixed in, would ever come to the truth about God by reason alone."[56]

With these words, the "Angelic Doctor", St. Thomas Aquinas, put his finger on an obvious problem. People, made for a God-like life of love but, in general, not "Listening" as described above, do not usually understand the meaning of life. They are not even very interested in it when they have the leisure to pursue it. Any lesser god, seeing such indifference, might get disgusted and chuck the whole enterprise. But the God of Love and the Incomprehensible Explosion decided to do something that would save the situation. That God decided to make a great Revelation, and to do so

---

[56] "…necessarium fuit hominem instrui revelatione divina quia veritas de Deo per rationem investigate, a paucis hominibus, et per longum tempus et cum admixtione multorum errorum provenit." Thomas Aquinas., <u>Summa Theologica</u>, Ia, I,1, cor.

without interfering with human freedom. "The Word became flesh and dwelt among us."

Persons of religious commitment are quite familiar with the notion of Order being the province of God. Jews, Christians, Muslims, all recognize God as the Ruler of the Universe. Reflective followers of Jesus of Nazareth may understand this directional unfolding of the universe even more sympathetically since it forms a basic part of their belief system. They already acknowledge that things and people were made for God. However, they do not always recognize this in their own Sacred Writings. To take a simple example, the first verses of the Gospel of John say, "In the beginning was the Word, and the Word was with God, and the Word was God. He was in the beginning with God; all things were made through Him and without Him was not anything made that was made."[57] The words seem clear enough. The Order found in the unfolding of the Cosmos is seen in the Christian Bible as "The Word." It is personified as a member of the Trinity, the Three-Persons-in-One God. Even at that long-ago moment, "In him was life, and the life was the light of humankind. The light shines in the darkness and the darkness has not overcome it."[58] The shift to the present tense in "shines" is deliberate, indicating the ongoing and constant source of the universe's existence.

That this Word is part of <u>everything</u> is stated with what is known as Semitic repetition.[59] When among Semitic people you say the same thing twice in a row, 'All was made through Him' and 'Without Him was made

---

[57] <u>The New Testament</u>, Gospel of St. John, 1,1-3 (Revised Standard Version).
[58] <u>Ibid.</u>, vv.4-5. Also, RSV except that I have translated "ανθρωπων" "humankind" instead of "men."
[59] This brief treatise is one of conclusions without lengthy explanations. Persons familiar with the use of literary genre, original languages, and every other tool they can get their hands on, will understand the emphasis being used here. Semitic repetition is a literary device commonly found in the ancient Near East.

nothing that was made', you mean it <u>really</u> emphatically. But if mankind evolves from the beginning and comes on the scene very late (modern science), and if the Word was in and through the process from the beginning and somehow the very 'light' of humankind (the Christian Scriptures), a merging of Order and The Word appears to be a happy coincidence. This should not be a problem for Christian believers since their Sacred Writings say clearly that the Word was in all things from the beginning. What can become a problem is bringing to the text a fundamental world view that insists that God make things complete, all at once, and separately from the cosmic process. The Christian scriptures never say this in so many words unless it is obviously using figurative language, but people who lack imagination tend to think literally and force literalism upon the text.[60] The people who wrote long ago were far from literalists.

John's opening words go on to say, "The Word became flesh, and dwelt among us." This Word through Whom all was made is identified as Jesus of Nazareth, bearing "light" for the world and yet the very same One, The Word, through Whom the world was made. God becomes human and tells people that they were made to be God's children. Through the love He will show them, they can become intimate with God through the friendship which He offers. The power to become such an intimate with God comes with "believing" in Him. This does not mean merely admitting that Jesus was Word of God, but it means accepting Him as the Way to live with God. The ancient meaning of "believe", is "trusting in his power", the same power of Order that made all things, and trusting it to bring a person to God. In addition, believing in Him does <u>not</u> make one a child of God, but gives one

---

[60] I say "obviously figurative" like the Creation Myth. One can hardly have real "evening and morning, one day" "days" before a "sun", a primary element for a "day", is ever made.

"the power <u>to become</u> a child of God" (τεκνα Θεου γενεσθαι). One must exercise the power of Christian love to become intimate with God.

This also means accepting and living His definition of Love: to engage yourself in the service of others. He explains that He is giving one, new commandment, "…that you love one another as I have loved you."[61] Then He proceeds to illustrate the "as I" by dying for his friends. Followers are to love, even to death if necessary. His teachings end up full of paradoxes: in giving you get, in losing you find, in dying you live. Humans are challenged by Jesus of Nazareth (The Word of God) to see life as a temporary stint. This is not a real problem since all can see that they all die anyway! During that stint they are to use their talents to serve others, so that all can grow into their true selves, personal centers within their own unique Order. Even as people are perfecting their talents, they are to do so in order to offer them to others – and certainly not to acquire power. This proper attitude is referred to by Jesus as living according to "The Spirit of God." As one might expect from one person of a single Three-Person-God, this is also referred to as Christ's own life.

The doctrine of the Trinity meshes well, to say the least, with the scientific unfolding and gathering of the Universe. The one God of Christianity is a gathering of three persons, where personhood is a "face", one of three living "faces" of the One God. The root meaning of "persona" is "face." This Communal, One Being is dynamically generative, consisting of the Father Person, who eternally begets the Son Person, with the Holy Spirit being the Love, another Person, eternally existing dynamically

---

[61] Jn.15,12.

between the Father and the Son, the Son and the Father.[62] The Unity of God exists in spite of the threefold Persons because it is not in time or space but is the Author of time and space.

So a Gathering exists as the Source of the Cosmos. The Cosmos comes forth and reveals itself to be an explosion emanating into 13.7 billion years of time and space. While it starts as an outward emanation, the Cosmos shows immediate signs of Gathering and Centering. Moreover, the longer it runs its course, the more gathered and complex the exploding pieces become, even gathering humans who can become persons themselves. The most advanced humans turns out to be the ones who love the most, gather closest with their fellow humans in cooperation, sharing, and mutual love. The more they love, the more they unite, peculiarly resembling the Source of the Incomprehensible Explosion. They do this uniting, in Christian terms, by reason of the Word of God through Whom all was made right from the beginning, and ends up being the God-life that enters into humans and, perfected, makes them Lovers like God – and like God able to escape the entropy of time and space.

We have said in the body of this treatise that persons who love are very different from people who do not. The Christian tradition insists that persons who "belong to Christ" are so different that they have undergone a completely new birth and "died" to their old self. They have "put on Christ" in a manner that makes them completely "reborn." The passages in the sacred writings indicating this are numerous.

---

[62] "Eternally" is one of the words that must be used, but about whose meaning little is known. Physicists almost universally agree that "time" is a creature, a dimension of things that move in space. "Eternal" is being, but not being in time and not having, as Aristotle noted of time, "a before and after."

What seems to be clear, if we may generalize, is that the follower of Christ will <u>not</u> decide on his or her own, like Adam and Eve did, but will listen to the Voice of Christ within, directing decisions to lead to what is most loving. This will probably not be as humans might guess them to be, but as God knows them to be (Jn.6, 45). This guidance is what is prayed for in the Lord's Prayer: "thy will be done", "lead us not into temptation", and "deliver us from evil."

Saint Paul, caught up in the same mysterious insight into life, said some very strange-sounding things. He noted that, "He (Jesus Christ) is the image of the invisible God, the first-born of all creation; for in him all things were created, in heaven and on earth, visible or invisible…all things were created through him and for him. He is before all things and in him all things hold together." (Col.1,15ff.) Of course, Christ is God or, in the personal language of the Trinity, has "equality with God."[63] So everything is made, according to Saint Paul, "for him" (his own words, εις αυτον, more like "towards him"). The Word is "before" (προ, "ante") the beginning, is <u>involved in</u>, and is <u>in</u> everything that is made, and is that towards which all tends.

Christian sages make much of Saint Paul's quote of the Greek philosopher, Epimenides, that in God, "…we live and move and have our being"(<u>Acts</u> 17,28). The "move" part is what fascinates them since Paul seems to say that everyday activities require the supportive force of God. A most basic form of the sin of pride, then, would be a human being making important decisions without prayer.

Death, Paul teaches, is the portal through which we go to join with Christ in a new life with God – if we love like him. He, Christ, Himself, gives us

---

[63] Cf. Phil.2,5ff. "…Christ Jesus, who, though he was in the form of God, did not count equality with God a thing to be grasped, but emptied himself…being born in the likeness of men."

the power to love in addition to offering His own life for us when He did not have to do it. This perfect example of love, to lay down your life for your friends, even not too friendly ones, is presented by Him to God the Father as a peace offering so that human failures to love will be overlooked. This was like saying, "So, they tortured me. I love them anyway. If I can forget it, You can forget the insults to You and the crimes against Your other children that they do."

Peace between God and Man is assured. This state of affairs, expressed in one form or another with conditions of belief attached, is also referred to as "The Good News", also known as "The Gospel."

Loving enemies is an invitation to love beyond what is normally understood as "reasonable." Jesus invites his followers to the next level of evolution. He offers them his own Spirit to give them the strength to live it. He wants to change his people and through them to change the world. He knows that love, especially of malicious, destructive people, is the only cure for them.

So, he asks his followers to begin by forgiving everyone for any past abuses, and to act with care and concern for all people as if they were ones own family members – something, Jesus insisted, and which we now know, they are. This loving behavior will, as in Jesus' own case, usually end up with the loving person injured or dead. However, the objects of their love change for the better, though usually some time after they have snapped back at the one loving them. Jesus said that, when struck on the cheek, true followers turn the other cheek, but he apparently knew that they would be struck on it as well. Change usually occurs only after the damage is done.

This is why the cross and, even more, the crucifix, have become the enduring symbols of Christianity.

Forgiveness of others is, of course, a natural corollary of being forgiven by God – even a prerequisite. Far easier to do in theory than in practice, forgiveness transforms the heart. (Some must begin by forgiving themselves!) God's heart is apparently so forgiving that becoming human and getting crucified was far more of an option than seeing "justice" done. "An eye for an eye" has no place in the new commandment of Jesus of Nazareth.

In passing we must note that the loving attitude expected of a Christian towards those who abuse him or her, does not extend in the same passive way to observing those abusing someone else. While Jesus of Nazareth is physically only found attacking the money changers in the Temple, those abusing his Father's house, he regularly warned people of the ultimate justice exacted by his Father in the next life. He goes so far as to say that everyone who is even angry with his (or her) brother will be liable to judgment (Mt.5,22). Followers are to be very slow to defend themselves with force, but quick to help others. In the presence of the prescription to "Love your neighbor as yourself", and in the absence of any instructions on how far to go, Christians are usually left with their own interpretation of how far is far enough to help ones neighbor or to intervene to prevent abuse. Some would say, though you must turn your own other cheek when set upon, you go "to the death" to save your neighbor from abuse. This, however, is pure speculation and each person is the sole judge of themselves before God.

The one, most consistent theme about Jesus of Nazareth that all scholars agree on is that he preached the coming of "The Kingdom of God." He taught the public always in parables, and most of them described the "Kingdom." It was like a woman who lost a coin, a grain of mustard seed, or a sower of seeds. It was like a pearl of great price or a man hiring laborers or holding a big wedding feast. From various points of view, different in each parable, Jesus preached that the Kingdom was coming and consisted of people who had recognized that God is the one who has made people as His children, and they are to live with one another in a just and generous manner as brothers and sisters. At the end, God will sort how well they have lived the trial, and then set up with them the Eternal Kingdom. All the people of the Earth are equally invited to join (much to the surprise of his Jewish apostles, especially Peter), and he sends them on a mission to tell everyone the Good News of God's friendship and to remind them of the loving way they must live.

St. Paul seems to suggest that those who do not join in the process of loving could perhaps be caught by entropy. He worries about people getting "free from the bondage of decay" but ends up hinting that, by a special act of the Creator, the whole of creation will end up escaping entropy. He also indicates that, according to his insight, the process is long and hard, not simple and easy. Nobody gets a free ride. He says,

"I consider that the sufferings of this present time are not worth
comparing with the glory that is to be revealed to us. For the creation waits with eager longing for the revealing of the sons of God; for the creation was subjected to futility …. The creation itself will be set free from its bondage to decay and obtain the glorious liberty of the children of God. We know the whole creation has been groaning in travail

together until now.... If we hope for what we do not see, we wait for it with patience." Rom.8,18ff.

For Paul, what is to be is already begun. He and we are waiting for its full appearance. Incidentally, in keeping with the usual fate of the really mature, the Romans cut his head off for preaching Christian love. Rome was inherently threatened by a theology that said that armed conquest was evil and became most anxious to stamp out Christianity. It did not work. However, armed conquest persists to this day as a favorite means of some world leaders to secure their desired order.

As noted, Paul's vision goes far beyond getting persons 'to heaven.' He has the whole of creation yearning for a new state of existence and starting on it immediately. For him, God's power, the Laws of Everything, The Word of God in everything, is, because of Christ, taking <u>everything</u> to a new heaven and a new earth. The Word of God, Jesus Christ, is also the Order that is in Things, that which holds them all together and keeps the process going in the direction towards Him who is both "the Alpha and the Omega, who is, who was, and who is to come." (Rev.1,8)

Considering that the description of the unfolding of the universe has been an understanding of science for only the last one hundred to one hundred and fifty years, the statements of the sacred texts are startling. All almost two thousand years old and describing a universe of unfolding growth towards a new way of living, they appear at least presentient. A scientist coming on the words, no matter what his or her religion or absence of it, could hardly ignore being impressed by them.

Everything said earlier about Order can be inferred from the New Testament under the notion of the activity of the Word or Spirit of God. Everything referred to in the discussion of the Someone – the Orderer – is consistent with the New Testament's understanding of God. The Laws of Everything are found in perfection in the New Testament's notion of God – where God is a Gathering of Three, but so perfectly gathered as to be only One. When God speaks, one voice speaks, but in the plural. "Let us make Man," God is presented as saying, "in Our image and likeness." God utters "The Word of God" and the Universe happens. It happens "for Him."[64]

This incredibly fascinating God revealed in the words of the New Testament turns out to be One, but a "Community of Three Persons" one of whom becomes man. This latter "Only begotten Son of God" ($\mu o \nu o \gamma \varepsilon \nu \eta s$) reveals that the Someone-Who-Made-Us loves us, and loves us so that He is willing to suffer and die as a human to show how much we are loved by the Communal One called God. At the same time, He points us toward the meaning of life – to love God and one another, to the death. The mind boggles. The lonely, absolute God of other monotheistic religions is overshadowed and reduced to a primordial concept. The fundamental reason why the basic law of the Universe is "Gathering", and why love is its finest expression, is revealed. The relation of Creator to creature is one of love deeper than humans can imagine. Love, itself, is the very nature of the

---

[64] We use the word "him" because we have no convenient pronoun. God is not him/her/it but produced them all.

Communal God. Bringing Forth, Gathering and Unifying, the basic principles of the evolving universe, emerge directly from the Nature of the Maker.

The general problem of pervasive competition and dominance after humans became self-destructive, Christianity explains under the notion of "Original Sin." In the first pages of the Bible humankind is shown to disobey the laws of God and be relegated to their own devices, "knowing the difference between good and evil" – and choosing the evil. This is handed down in Christian tradition as the "Fall." Put simply, "Something is wrong with humans." They have an internal flaw that not only <u>allows</u> them to make choices, merely human freedom, but seems to invite them to ignore the Order in and around them and make <u>bad</u> choices. In terms of modern cosmology, at least one theologian, Matthew Fox, described this flaw more as a "failure to rise." The developing humans, having reached the point of being able to act unselfishly on behalf of their fellow humans, decided to look out for themselves at the expense of their neighbors. They "fell", in the sense that they failed to embrace that love which would move them to a new, higher level.

Also consistent with our observations above, about love being the work of Order and evil being the work of people getting in the way of Order, is the basic Christian theological position on good works. No man, these theologians say, can earn "heaven" – it is the gift of God. If humankind does good, it has only done what it is inclined in its nature to do and should thank God for its goodness. If humankind does evil, it should cry out for forgiveness, because it has derailed the natural purposes of the Creator. God alone is good; humankind is responsible for all evil.

The Gospel of John also hints at the "inside" involvement of God in the whole process. When Jesus is chided by his opponents for healing on the Sabbath, he says mysteriously, "My Father is working still, and I am working." Our very staying in existence is the work of God. The text says this really angered his opponents because "he not only broke the Sabbath, but also called God his Father, making himself equal with God." (Jn.5,17-18)[65] Similarly, St. Paul notes that only one "Lord" exists, and only "…one God and Father of us all, who is above all, and through all and in all (έις Θεὸς…ὁ ἐπι πάντων και δια πάντων και εν πασιν. Eph.4,6), just like the Word.

People generally are not given much credit. Having enough of a receptive mind even to listen to Jesus is attributed by Jesus to his Father's hand as taught by the prophet, Isaiah, "They shall all be taught by God" (Jn.6,45). Later, at his last supper with his disciples, he will tell them that he will send the Holy Spirit Who will dwell in them after he is gone, and that Spirit will lead them in the ways of "all truth." Even discovering the truth is attributed to the dynamic Order working inside each person, and is not due to any special greatness on their part. God is to be thanked for everything. Humankind beats its breast for the trouble it causes.

We now know the reason why people are not given much credit. They have evolved and bear traces of their evolution. They naturally concern themselves with survival and what they consider a very important concept,

---

[65] Cf. also, Heb.1,2-3: "…a Son…through whom also he [God] created the world. He [the Son] reflects the glory of God and bears the very stamp of his nature, upholding the universe by his word of power."

"Justice." But these notions clash with true love, their more ultimate goal. Hence, they must constantly decide what is just, but then decide whether something more loving can be put into effect. For example, murderers cannot be allowed to go free. However, among Christians they should not be executed. They need to be fed, housed, clothed, and incarcerated in the loving hope that, before they die, they might become loving persons. Love may help even them reach the purpose of their existence.

Many, upon hearing things like this transcendence beyond justice, will say, 'That is foolish.' One must always remember that it is written, "The foolishness of God is wiser than the wisdom of men." I Cor.1,25

But persons of faith are to play a direct role in the spread of the truth and the building up of the Kingdom. "To each a gift of the Spirit is given for the good of everyone else", says Paul (I Cor.12,7). We spoke above how, by following ones bliss, one discovers the special gift that is ones own. Putting the gift to use never seems to lack opportunity, though the discovery and the willingness to use it for others seems more hard won.

The ultimate purpose of God is to make the truly loving being, the "person" spoken of above, and through that person the blossoming of others. The Word of God, Jesus of Nazareth, referred to himself as "the Vine", to us as "the Branches", and to God, the Father, as the "Vinedresser." We are "pruned" by the events of life, to become ever more loving, and these are led by God.[66] We are constantly being challenged to grow more and more until we die. We are also "pruned" by what we learn and, hence, these pages. As Jesus said, "You are already pruned because of the word that I spoke to you."[67]

---

[66] Jn.15,1-8.
[67] Ibid.

Many variants of Christianity have sprung up over the centuries, and both wars and persecutions have come from their arguments with one another. What seems to have emerged is that most forms contain great kernels of truth, capable of transforming people into persons. But all seem to fail when they limit "salvation" either to their own membership or to their own formulae, thus apparently limiting the evolutionary and saving power of God. They especially need to remember that when Jesus said, "No one comes to the Father except by Me" He did not say that the person coming to the Father would know that He got there because of Jesus.

Religions made from formulae are especially dangerous. Christianity was not meant to be a "religion" in the sense of "methods to get you to Heaven." Christianity was meant to be a collectivity of people who were imbued with, and guided by, the Spirit of God, each using his or her own special gifts. Christianity is a collective Spirituality. Some subtle point exists, a temptation in all Christian's lives, where one might settle for doing all the little "duties" of religion instead of meditating daily on the direction one is being called, and called uniquely, by the Spirit of God.

As one sage noted, "Religion is for those who do not want to go to hell. Spirituality is for those who have been there and don't want to go back." This was originally said by a Jesuit priest who taught Bill Wilson how to live. Bill, in turn, founded "Alcoholics Anonymous", the most potent spiritual force during the twentieth century after Jesus.

Another mysterious passage of the New Testament says, "His divine power has granted to us all things that pertain to life and godliness....he has granted to us his precious and very great promises, that through these you may escape from the corruption that is in the world ... and become partakers of the divine nature." (II Pet.1,3-4) In the New Testament, believers are seen as escaping into a new life that belongs only to God – the kind of "being" that already was before "The Incomprehensible Explosion." Unlike our analysis above, or the Noosphere of Teilhard de Chardin, the New Testament does not simply offer the next world as an inevitable place to which all are going whether they are aware of it or not. Rather, those go there who live according to the Way and Promises of Jesus, led by Him. Persons were actually made "for Him" from the beginning, according to the New Testament, and the absolutely final word that can be said about, "Why are we?" is claimed by the same sacred text as, "To be friends of the Living God." We require generation by parents and preparation by life and its trials and tribulations. But, in the end, we join God as friends.

And some Christians believe that <u>all</u> will be guided by God, the Orderer inside of us, and <u>all</u> will end up "saved" by the Savior of all. In one well-worn passage of the Bible Jesus, when asked when He will restore the Kingdom of God, replies, "The Kingdom of God is within you." That is to say, 'It isn't <u>coming</u>, it is growing out from within.' He will lead everyone "home" and we will <u>all</u> meet again. In the words of the poet, John Henry Newman, in his poem, "Lead Kindly Light:

> So long Thy power hath blessed me, sure it still
>   Will lead me on,
> O'er moor and fen, o'er crag and torrent till
>   The night is gone;
> And with the morn those angel faces smile
> Which I have loved so long since, and lost
>   Awhile.

However optimistically some would read the Christian sacred texts, they clearly say God gathers everyone together for a judgment of each life, after death. Jesus, the Christ, refers to it only once, but it is a highly significant passage (Mt.25). Once everyone is gathered the division of good from evil will be based on what people did for each other during their lives. He says that he, himself, is in every person, an echo of what John's Gospel and Paul said. As a result, whatever anyone did for other persons, they did for him and, thus, for God – like feeding them when they were hungry, or visiting them when they were in prison. Similarly, he says whatever they did not do, when they obviously should have, is a failure to love and earns one rejection. Life is about loving, and love is about helping any and all other people. These other people have within them the Word of God that has come from God and is developing towards God. All people are free to do whatever they want, but they neglect care of others at the peril of missing the point of life itself – and perhaps earning retribution.[68]

The people who gather around the message of Jesus are called by Him, "the Church." Lost in history is the precise structure of the gathering of these persons. The various sects of Christianity argue vehemently to this day about exactly what the structure of the Church as Institution ought to be. Some say one must join this or that sect or never achieve human destiny. Others say that is an invention of the churches to hold their members. However one puts together the tenets of Christianity, the openness to achieve "heaven" must be there for absolutely everyone achieving personhood, coming before or after Christ, knowing about Christ or not knowing about Him, otherwise the obvious nature of God, Absolute Love, is violated. This does not mean any person has ever earned heaven.

In Christianity it is quite clear that no one achieves their destiny because they perfectly met all the challenges of life. All will finally need some forgiveness promised by the crucified Savior. The tradition for this extends

---

[68] On one occasion, John the Baptist warns some hypocritical followers about "the wrath to come", referring to the judgment, Christianity says, all must undergo (Mt..3,7).

back to many hundreds of years before Jesus when it was observed that no human could stand before God if he or she were honestly judged. St. Paul also adds that no one can ever plead ignorance of Order because,

> "…ever since the creation of the world his invisible nature, namely his eternal power and deity, has been clearly perceived in the things that have been made" (Rom.1,20).

On the other hand, The God of Christianity's sacred writings loves all creation, and goes through considerable pains to gather everyone in. As the Poet Hopkins, in the poem already cited, notes about God's world,

> "There lives the dearest freshness deep down thing…because the Holy Ghost over the bent world broods with warm breast and with, ah! bright wings."

In a comprehensive statement about the Gathering of Everything, one final quote from the Bible is worth considering. In a letter of John (I,4) it reads: "…God is love, and he who abides in love abides in God, and God in him." God does not "have" love, the way we do, any more than God has existence the way we do. On the contrary, God simply "Is" and "Is Love" -- it is we who participate in it according to our commitment and dedication. Centuries before John wrote this passage, when Moses asked God's name so that he could answer the Egyptians if they questioned him, God said, "I AM. Tell them 'I AM' sent you."

Finally, recalling an old legend about St. John, the author of the gospel, is appropriate here. In his great old age he is reported to have given up trying to explain Christianity to people and merely repeated over and over to all who approached him, "Little children, love one another."

From another viewpoint, the Bible leaves quite open whether people can or cannot develop further as humans in this life. Now we have the capacity to think reflectively and to love unconditionally. That we might, as individuals and/or as a species, obtain a more effective capacity to do these things, is left quite open. That we might all attain a state of being with photographic memories, extrasensory perceptions, telepathic communications, or all have some of the strange gifts of mathematics or memory found only in savants, is not affirmed or denied. That we might attain a level of consciousness that enables us to "see" the world immediately and totally as the magical, mythical, mysterious product of the Unseen God – apparently the way Jesus of Nazareth saw it – remains a possibility. After all, in referring to his "mighty works", or "miracles", Jesus told his followers, "Greater works than these will [my followers] do" (Jn.14,12), and we do not seem to have gotten there yet. The power probably comes with the advanced perception we are too primitive to see.

That we will pass on to another state of being in a life after this one is clearly taught. That at least some, and maybe all, will be in a new state of union with the God Who made them is insisted upon, including keeping our particular individuality while at once being in perfect unity with God. In the sacred texts of Christians, living is no trivial pursuit but a matter of ultimate concern.

All religious persons need to take another hard look at what they are saying about God. They must examine their sacred texts carefully and make certain that they are not violating the obvious conditions of the origins of the human race.[69] The Maker seems to love everyone equally – and statements to the contrary are made at the peril of the one making the statement.

---

[69] In the Roman Catholic Church, Pope Pius XII, in 1943 in his encyclical, <u>Divino Afflante Spiritu</u>, warned Catholic biblical interpreters that they "…must not contradict the certain conclusions of modern science." God is also the Author of Science.

Parents generally take a dim view of people who say nasty things about their children. God, whose children we are, might not like it either.

In conclusion, the scientific findings about the meaning of the Universe are in marvelous agreement with a theistic philosophy and traditional Christian teachings. (We are not including, of course, those groups, always on the fringe of Christianity, who pick up the Bible, ignore its original languages, ignore the human errors evident in its pages, skip over the mountains of evidence of its edited and compiled nature, and treat it like a book of divine dictation, literal history, and/or magical predictions.) The terms used are sometimes different and emphasis on "direction" in science turns into "design" in philosophy and "God" in Christianity. But they are all the same, and they complement each other to give direction to any human beings no matter where they start their search. For the Seeker, an answer to the question of "Why?" is available in every direction, but it does require a willingness to pursue an answer. Some find it in the orderly movement of the galaxies, some find it in the crystals of cooling lava, and some find it in the beauty of lives well lived. But it is available to all if, wherever one starts, one persists with care, listens deep inside, and overlooks none of the Beauty that "flames out, like shining from shook foil."

III. METHOD

At this point we must talk about "method" because Why? questions require a different sort of answer than a description of what has happened in the Universe since the Incomprehensible Explosion, or even a description of the direction it has taken. Moreover, because the last couple of centuries have been dominated by the "scientific method", other viable forms of inference have been placed in some mistrust.

One of the first characteristics of humans with the ability of reflex self-awareness is the ability to discover and describe things that are not "there." Things like Hate and Love cannot be seen, heard, tasted, touched or smelled, but they are. As a matter of fact, they are some of the most important things in life, though a laboratory may be quite useless for their discovery. People have lost their lives to the justice system simply because of Motive. Armies frequently march out of Hatred or Greed. These are not abstractions. They are easily and readily discovered by those who look for them carefully – and, like the atom, they are known primarily from their effects upon the sensible world we live in. Unlike the atom, they do not even have the potential of being physically measured or observed.

They are like the Black Holes of space, so obvious to the astronomers. Black Holes were discovered, as was our planet Neptune, because they had a gravitational pull on something we did know about. They are realities that are sometimes never directly measured or observed, but are inferred from their indirect confrontations with us. (Later Neptune was easily photographed but, in the sense of collecting the light that comes from an object onto a sensitive plate, it is impossible to photograph a black hole.) Some of these realities we may never learn all about because we may never get to meet them head on, but that does not stop us from declaring their existence and often being able to write whole books about them. We might say as a principle, 'Whatever is observed that is not self-explanatory has its explanation in something else.'

Books can be written because unobservable traits of an unobserved reality can be as "visible" in the real world as the effects produced by the unobserved. Think about a murderer who realizes his wife is going to tell authorities of his illegal activities and so he has an accomplice kill her. The accomplice is caught and fingers the murderer. The murderer is convicted without a single measurable or observable connection to the crime beyond the say-so of a known murderer – and Motive. The man is in prison for life. He was convicted because of visible murder done out of fear, a trait in him not noticed by anyone, and like himself, a reality completely absent from the crime scene except in its effect.

Sometimes when you have examined a scene thoroughly and you believe you have all of the elements that put the scene there, you "feel" something is missing. As in the case mentioned above, the scene's perpetrators all gathered together had no <u>motive</u>. Even crimes by madmen are never completely senseless because even their madness has a twisted logic. The ultimate criminal was discovered and firmly linked to the crime scene by the motive, absent from all the other elements but necessary for a complete understanding of the scene. Without the Motive, the scene made no "sense", and that was so unacceptable to the investigators that they would not stop their search. Our scene remains disturbing to us – admittedly with some more disturbed than others – until we fathom why it is here, and why we are in it.[70]

Different scenes with searches for different items have different results, though the inferences used may be similar, or even identical. A tiger can kill a native and the tiger, while it may be hunted down and killed, is not guilty

---

[70] The philosopher, Bernard Lonergan, once described a human being, in so far as (s)he is human, as "a pure, unadulterated desire to know."

of anything. "Guilt" cannot be attributed to tigers, except by metaphor. Why? Because "Guilt", an invisible, but sometimes real element in the discovery of a criminal, is only attributed to people who can design actions freely. Discovering a violently killed person tells us, "A killer exists somewhere." A review of the scene may reveals pages and pages about the totally unobserved killer. If a human murderer, it may reveal even details like the height, weight, and sex of the perpetrator, so much that he is easily caught. If a tiger was the killer, seen from foot and claw prints, missing parts may tell observers why: "It was hungry." In a recent California death by a lion, the question why was answered by footprints at the scene: "The jogger got between the lion and its cubs."

This kind of inference, arguing from the known effects to the existence and nature of the one causing the effects, is the kind of argumentation that must be used to answer the question of why we are here – if a Why exists. The cosmic scene is examined and the "direction" of things is observed, an unfolding to the ever more complicated and centered. The Laws governing the unfolding, Gathering, Centering, Complicating, are worked out. Beauty and Truth are found. They <u>must</u> have an explanation. Incredible meshing of seemingly unrelated spheres is found to produce the Biosphere. The latest products of the Biosphere, humans, are examined and the story of their development through some form of evolution or intelligent unfolding to intelligent, free persons is noted. "Intelligent", "free", "person", all parts of the Scene, must have an explanation. From all of this we may infer some things about "The Universe" or "Order" or "The Order Behind the Universe." The name is irrelevant. What we are looking for is What or Who arranged the scene, and Why.

We are reasonably sure that Who would be better than What because the Scene contains persons. If the Scene has them, they had to be, in some form or other, in the explosion that caused the Scene, or in the Scene Arranger, heretofore called Order. Similarly, Power. If atoms are little bundles of pent-up power ($E=MC^2$), then Power had to be available to their Arranger. Like a crime scene, the Universe is Our Gift Scene – for life is a great gift – and, like a crime scene, must contain Our Truth and answer our questions about our origin, direction and meaning.

When we ask, "Why are we?", we are asking a different question than the one asked by all the wonderful physicists and cosmologists from Isaac Newton through Albert Einstein and the contemporary, Steven Hawking. Their "Why?" question involves the nature of the forces that brought us from the Incomprehensible Explosion – one of their great discoveries – to here. The difference can be illustrated. When a forensic analyst asks, "Why is this body dead?" a complete answer might well be, "Because of blunt force trauma to the head of at least fifty foot/pounds at the point of impact." For the detective this is interesting and helpful information, but his "Why is this body dead?" requires a completely different answer. His question, "Whodunit?" is classic. In our gift-scene, the physicists are the forensic analysts. We are the detectives. The limitations of their equipment, while producing wonderful evidence and clues, do not give them answers to our questions except in forms of, to them, unreliable inductive inferences.

These observations about method are extremely important for the human race. The dominance of the scientific method for the last several hundreds of years has left us with an attitude towards philosophical and theological principles that makes them, as Professor Michael Behe put it, "...at root, chosen by the individual."[71] True as that is, one would hate to have such persons investigate ones murder. Having arrived at a circumstantial description of the agent of death, complete with precise measurements of blunt force trauma or grams of poison, such investigators might reach the limit of their methodology. The murderer would not be caught because no 'real proof', in their eyes, could be forthcoming. "Live And Let Live" would be the end of the story even though someone would have died.[72]

While admitting that a great danger exists in insisting on the truth of ones evidence – occasionally someone is unjustly accused – I believe that not insisting on such truth carries a greater danger – too many murderers go free and an attitude of 'you can get away with it' spreads through the community. To have people go through life with a strange notion of God because theological principles are merely 'a matter of individual preference' is tragic as we know from the spectacle of Jonestown.[73]

Far more importance rests around coming to agreement about methodological principles of philosophy than of science, especially as scientific progress shrinks the world. When people are forced by progress to live cheek-by-jowl with persons of different persuasions, the philosophical and theological disagreements are far more likely to cause real trouble than the scientific ones. Science, carefully interpreting the crude experiences of humankind, always provides much of the refined evidence needed for good philosophy. This is a great responsibility. If the progress of science can

---

[71] Behe, p.250.
[72] Ibid.
[73] In Guyana, South America, in November of 1978, the Rev. Jim Jones, occasionally proclaiming that he was, in fact, Jesus of Nazareth, had four persons killed, including a Congressman investigating the welfare of some of his constituents. Jones then announced "The End" and led his followers, most from San Francisco, California, in a bizarre murder/suicide of 912 of them, including more than 200 children.

show clearly a "Designed Unfolding", then to do so is of the utmost importance in the discussion of life and its meaning because it might reveal a direction of unfolding and a necessary philosophical principle of living.

Moreover, in the matter of philosophical and theological principles, the truth cannot be decided by a jury of twelve, but must be decided by everyone interested in it – and in some peculiar way, that means everyone. As Socrates observed, truth is not a matter of counting heads. But neither is it a matter of indifference. Left alone with the scientific method, or even believing it to be a superior way of approaching life, the human is severely hampered in the basic abilities to arrive at the most important truths of living.[74] Allowing a murderer to go free is a trifle compared to allowing someone with a morally baseless or indifferent attitude to have an unchallenged position of influence in the lives of the people of the world.

Once having examined the process from there to here and seeing the Order and complexity of the unfolding, one does not defy logic in any way by making predictions about from here to hereafter. Natural Science does it all the time. The one thing that Natural Science can then do is to verify the prediction by experiment. This backup procedure is not available to the philosopher or theologian. He or she is left in the position of scientists <u>before</u> the existence of atom was proved out, and before the first atomic bomb was exploded. He or she is left with making tightly reasoned arguments and making warnings, with total personal conviction but without mathematical demonstration, "Stand way back!"

---

[74] For the variety of methods of inference, cf., Lonergan, Bernard, <u>Insight, A Study in Human Understanding</u>. The Philosophical Library: New York, 1957. Cf. also, Smith, Huston, <u>Why Religion Matters: The Fate of the Human Spirit in an Age of Disbelief</u>. Harper: San Francisco, 2001

For most of us human seekers of meaning, like most of the observers before the first atomic explosion at Alamogordo, New Mexico – and even some of the scientists – some faith is involved. To those unable to grasp the subtleties of the demonstration, a leap must be made from the gathered data and its implications for the final heuristic structure proposed. For Albert Einstein, and very few others, no surprises occurred in New Mexico.

With the appearance of humans, knowledge of the direction and source of the cosmos becomes knowable and, as far as we Earthlings are concerned, knowable for the first time. But, as the Philosopher, Aristotle, noted, the answer to the question Why? about any event or scene is usually the very last thing that one can discover but, known as the "Final Cause", it is the only thing that can really explain the thing or event.

An example is in order here. Suppose you arrive like the famous native, Ishi, from the Stone Age into downtown San Francisco in the early part of the 20th century.[75] You come across a construction site where a sky-scraper is being built. You decide to watch one of the workers very closely. He arrives with his lunch pail and works all day, every day, putting up girders, riveting and other such tasks. You ask, "Why is he doing all this?" When you see the finished building, you say, "This is why the man was working." When you see the building filled with new tenants, maybe some living in apartments, and some setting up business offices, you say, "This is why the man was working."

But you no longer see the man. Where is the man? You investigate and discover that he is erecting another building a few blocks away. You seek

---

[75] Kroeber, Theodora, <u>ISHI in Two Worlds: A Biography of the Last Wild Indian in North America</u>.
University of California Press: Berkeley, 1961. Ishi was found in a remote part of northern California, near Oroville, in 1911. He died of tuberculosis in 1914.

him out and notice that he does not care at all for the building he has just built. You follow him home. He drives to San Mateo and goes every Friday to a bank and deposits a pay check. You say, "This is why he is working." You follow him home and see his house and his wife and children. Then you remember your early days in the tribe and the work done to form and care for your family. Then you say, with some finality, "This is why he is working." All that girder-climbing and riveting, so totally unrelated to raising a family, suddenly makes sense. They are part of a very complicated social network that escapes your stone-age mind – but the connectedness and good sense of each part emerges into clarity. You understand "family building" and your question, "Why?", while not totally resolved, is plausibly answered.

You have many questions about each of the items contributing to the man's care of his family – Where do rivets come from? How does one learn to rivet? Why build such tall buildings? – but you know they contribute to the final result of family building. Were you to examine rivets and riveting all by themselves, you would become hopelessly and endlessly lost in your attempt to answer, "Why does the man do this?" So, too, people who investigate the "Why?" of mankind always become totally lost when they examine in detail any one part of the picture.

When seeking the direction of a process, the moments along the way *as a series* reveal the direction, not the individual moments. Driving to work, riveting, depositing checks in the bank, none of these reveal anything about why the man is doing anything. But, taken all together, including the relation of each moment to the previous moment and all to the last moment, the family, reveals the direction, "Why." You know why people raise families and may even take it for granted. But somewhere, some of us will ask, "Why do you raise a family?" and your answer will lead to another why, and another why, and another until you ask the ultimate, "Why?" that is the question asked in this treatise: "Why are we?"

At this point in the discussion of method something must be said concerning the observation of Lamarck, Darwin, and other evolutionary scientists about the principles of our unfolding, such as, "Survival of the Fittest." This law for every species, noted by Darwin in the 19th Century and long before the great advances in physics and some significant cosmological discoveries, was an accurate observation of the inner Order of living things. He observed that they react to whatever they find in their environment and they change to survive. They may change color to hide from predators. They may grow larger fins to move faster and catch food.

Interestingly, they may change and become faster to catch their <u>favorite</u> food, even though they are fast enough already to get quite enough to eat. This latter kind of development, coming from the inner Order of the animal, is really quite different from an alteration merely to survive and might rather be called the "flowering", "maturation", or "perfecting" of the fittest. The source of this development is in the "consciousness" of the living thing, albeit on a pre-self-knowledge or instinctive level.

"Survival of the fittest", then, is an insight into one important inner working of the vast array of processes of the inner Order happening in living things. It is an important first step. However, it is but a tiny part of evolution and is restricted to living things. Especially after the 20th Century physical and cosmological discoveries and telescopic developments, like the Hubble Telescope, survival of the fittest appears as a secondary principle to survival of the most gathered and centered.

Even the latter principle seems to be nuanced in the unfolding by the elimination of some of the more gathered and centered, like various *homines erecti,* in favor of 'the most gathered and centered among a group of gathered and centered.' As already suspected by some scientists, whole species, quite fit for survival and further development, like dinosaurs, are seen to be "removed" by Nature as it apparently drives towards the more Gathering and Centering. Humans, far more gathered and centered, emerge, but could not have survived had they emerged at the same time as the dinosaurs.

In the context of questions about what Nature is doing, therefore, the principle of survival of the fittest seems to take second place to the survival of the most complicated, interiorized beings. This principle, in turn, takes a back seat to a deeper, more ultimate principle. That principle involves the reason Why? beings have become increasingly interiorized and centered and apparently has something to do with Spirituality and Spiritual Development. To say, "Nature is about Survival of the Fittest" is not wrong, but it is such a partial answer as to be almost meaningless.

In addition, "Survival" simply cannot be said of geological and geophysical formations, yet they, and the complicated spheres that come from them, play an absolutely essential role in the production of living things which, in turn, must then strive to survive. To try to say that nothing is happening in the evolution of mankind when whole spheres (Hydrosphere, Atmosphere, and so on) are being developed and, by their combination, make living things at all possible, is unreasonable. A taboo seems to exist that makes it importunate to say, "The production of the hydrosphere plays a very intelligent role in the evolution of living things" or "We are a product of a highly intelligent, internally managed unfolding." Reasonable method must finally triumph.

IV. HUMANS ALONE

As humans developed their conclusions about their own origin and direction, perhaps the most terrifying prospect was the emergence of the idea that they can influence, and possibly disrupt totally, the direction towards which the cosmos is unfolding – at least in their niche, the Earth. Obvious in several different sciences, studies show that humans affect not only the behavior of other humans, but may even affect what they pass along in their genes to their offspring. Could what people do have such a profound effect upon the universe? Could people given the gift of life in a totally mysterious, free, and equal manner disrupt the very process that gave them birth? Human notions, organizations, and behavior have certainly had their effects upon human history and must be considered in the Search.

A brief survey of some well-known human actions will give us at least a working picture of human frailty to help us get clear in our minds the kind and extent of the effects humans have upon their own development, especially if our unfolding shows a basic direction of gathering, complicating and interiorizing. We cannot look at ourselves with a critical eye unless we realize that we play an essential role in what life is all about and what it comes to be. Moreover, if we find that the role we play seems always to have negative elements, that fact would be a great incentive to investigate, discover and adopt, some other role and, perhaps, include spirituality and prayer.

The first thing we notice about people is that individuals can really make a difference in their own lives, and especially noticeable are the ones who make a mess of it. People who drink too much or try to get through life by, say, stealing, usually end up very badly, especially if they are poor. These same people make a great impact on their families, often impoverishing them. Statistically noticeable also is the number of children of these same unfortunates who end up the same way. They are not forced to – many do not – but many do. Enough do for us to be able to say statistically, "Poverty, violence and crime breed poverty, violence and crime." We can even generalize: "Dysfunctional behavior breeds dysfunctional behavior." We seem to teach our children by what we, ourselves, do.

The next thing we notice is that a great number of people acting in a self-destructive manner can cause the deterioration of a whole society. This is not to say that the deteriorating society notices its own deteriorating. If a solid majority drinks too much or steals or puts its trust in a golden calf or a bird-headed lion, then they all go down together. In cases where the populace is sufficiently naïve and uneducated and the leaders dysfunctional, the same result ensues.

The basis of self-destruction generally rests in the legitimate instincts for survival gone sour. All of us need food, clothing, shelter – the stuff of survival. And, with nomadic wandering ended, we need a reasonable amount of stuff for when we run short. But when we are forced to choose between the opportunity to get stuff we do not need, or stuff that quite legitimately belongs to someone else, we are faced with "morality", and our own free choice. The temptation to rationalize is enormous. We "need" the stuff, or "they" don't need it like we do. Maybe "they" don't deserve it like we do because they are the wrong color, religion, or attitude. Or maybe "they" just came by it too easy and we decide they shouldn't have it so easy. Here, in miniature, is the basis of almost all wars. War is always about "stuff." If a war appears not to be about stuff, merely look deeper or back in time a little, and the stuff will appear. A great deal of violence and dysfunctional behavior exist around sex, but the greater culprit is greed, especially when it extends beyond individuals to families and societies.

In other words, Societies can be like people. They can have, *en masse*, all the negative traits of individuals – and these in spite of what it says in their Constitutions. One country so declared that all men were created equal. However, they really did not mean "humans" as everyone thought, but "males", and did not include black men or any women. They said the words, but the leaders made laws that did not use the proper meaning of their terms, and devised all manner of deceptions to keep things confused. Moreover, in their hearts they always thought they had excellent reasons for not putting their own words fully into effect.

People have arrived at positions of authority and have become politicians. Then, guided by patriotism or racism, they have led whole nations astray. When such people rule, thousands can be murdered in very short spaces of time.[76] Similarly, philosophical or theological positions that ignore the observations about our Equality, our Origin and our Direction, instead espousing war and selfishness, should not go unchallenged by Science where at least the challenge of Intelligent Design can be clearly made. The whole truth will set us free from the burdens wrought by our mistakes concerning what life is all about.

---

[76] After the terrorist attack of September 11, 2001, in which 2800 people were killed because of theological disagreement, a war was initiated that killed more than 5,000 innocent people in Afghanistan by mid-December of that same year! This latter horror was primarily accomplished by very inaccurate "Carpet Bombing" from 30,000 feet so that the bombers would be too high to shoot down. When moral philosophers complained, they were told these innocent deaths were "necessary collateral damage."

Societies often follow their leaders, and the leaders, being human, always make mistakes. A civil war was fought in one human country to free the slaves, the real "stuff" behind that war. Yet, the "freed" slaves remained in a carefully constructed bondage for another hundred years, and in some sense still remain in bondage in spite of those who died for their freedom. Some of the leaders, and many of the people, did not want their freedom and made sure they did not obtain it.

Interestingly, people of a country who acquire more than, say, $50,000,000, in present day currency, already an absurd amount of wealth for any family,[77] will begin to talk like they are not acquiring more wealth, but "providing services." The owner of over a hundred condominiums will explain building another fifty as "providing housing." He or she will do this even as they evict tenants who cannot come up with increased rents because of misfortune, sickness and such. Anyone defending such people, and not able to see that this is a corruption of human life, has already missed the mysteriousness of the unfolding of life during our brief stay on Earth -- or, more likely, never saw the point in the first place. This is also true of persons who want to close the public schools because "they are too costly and inefficient." The same is true for those who say no taxes should be levied for anything except what helps them protect their wealth or gain more: police, armies and roads.

Wise men, speaking the language of love and beyond basic animal

---

[77] For a rule of thumb: If you could pile all of your private wealth into a heap of $100 bills and fall off of it and not hurt yourself, you are reasonably wealthy. If you would get killed, or even seriously hurt in the fall, you have way too much. For example, a ten foot stack is about $2.7 million dollars. You could hurt yourself and maybe should give some away. At 15 feet, right around $4 million, you <u>will</u> get hurt, and could kill yourself – at least your soul.

instincts, have for centuries pointed out that "Private Ownership" is not an absolute right.[78] If no one is responsible for his or her own existence on Earth, then no one is born with any rights to things different from anyone else's rights. Any alleged right, acquired later by law, must be viewed in the perspective of other people's needs. For example, what if William Penn had decided that, since he was given the deed to Pennsylvania, he would make it his private estate and no one else would be allowed in it? A very large clash of "rights" would have immediately occurred.

Viewed from the scientific position of the origin of the human race and the processes of its production, the Earth belongs to everyone. Just because this or that country decides on certain borders and a fiscal philosophy and monetary system that allows people to amass unlimited amounts of wealth does not mean that such a system is ethical or just. On the contrary, the nature of humanity often says that it is not. While industry, talent, and privilege may cause one person to acquire more things and property than another, the moment that property is *vitally needed* by any other person on Earth, and not so needed by the owner, the right to that property ceases. This is a simple, scientific conclusion from the basic facts of our evolution, if not from the fact that we are but one large family.

In a word, we do not put ourselves here, we find ourselves here. Legal and illegal may be based on law and its cases, but Good and Evil are based on inalienable rights fixed in our human origins. Simply put, if you are starving and I have plenty, I owe you.[79]

---

[78] See the path in the 13th Century of Thomas Aquinas, carefully drawn between ownership of use and absolute ownership: Summa Theologica, III^a, q.66, a.2, cor.
[79] Of course, if you are repeatedly or unwittingly starving, I may also need to educate you.

From another point of view, some people may never be impressed with being loved – we are truly free beings. Therefore, if a country is forced to take some money and/or property away from some of its citizens who have too much because, for example, millions of its children lack health care, the least it can do is award something like a "Medal of Freedom" to the ones from whom the excess wealth has been extracted. In severe cases, it might also erect a bust or even a whole statue and place it before the public extolling their "generosity." For some reason, this seems to placate the otherwise intractable animalism of their natures.

Societies try to hide their injustices, just like people. The treatment of Native Americans is a glaring example, especially the Cherokee "Trail of Tears" and the massacre at Wounded Knee. For decades the true story was absent from textbooks, and still gets little treatment. One state fought Mexico for independence – so that they might have slaves, contrary to the laws of Mexico, then a country that condemned slavery. They won their independence and established a slave state, but the truth of what they were fighting for is still absent from the public school history books of that State. The State claimed, in one of those wonderful ironies that sometimes occur in history, they were fighting for "freedom"!

However, no society will find a way to make sure that everyone is a loving person. Those who do not love will strain mightily to curb the generous tendencies of such a society. They will often repeat things like, 'I do not mind being charitable, but I, alone, will decide who to give my money to.' The society will need to enact laws that redistribute wealth since the misers and exploiters in it will try to acquire <u>everything</u> if they can. When this fact is not recognized, a society more or less gradually becomes what is now called "A Third World Country" – a country of a few very rich, who are the *de facto* rulers, and a vast number of the very poor. These rich are those at whom the sarcastic, but insightful T-shirt aims when it reads, "The one who dies with the most toys wins."

Even the best leaders the richest countries (like most of the world's leaders) have ever had, almost to a man, have put the interests of their own country ahead of other, equal, human beings to the extent that these others have been abused, sometimes impoverished, sometimes killed. Somehow having a nation-state has been understood to give license to its leaders to treat others as lesser than themselves – a position contrary to the evidence of the story of unfolding from the Incomprehensible Explosion, and often contrary to the very constitution of the nation-state. Life to each and every one of us is, simply and quite obviously, a gift. If human beings are ever to attain a "more human" or "beyond human" level, at least in the United States, they will need to find some way of looking at the world differently from that of the present nation-state. Perhaps they will also need to find leaders wholly other than the ones they now legitimatize.

In passing, and based upon the absolute equality of people before the mystery of entering this life, we note that a great deal more ways of getting things wrong appear than getting them right. For example, patriotism is not an absolute value and endorsing the words and/or policies of leaders is not *ipso facto* a good or admirable thing. The duty of every citizen is to weigh and measure the decision of his or her leaders carefully, not even in the light of the country's constitution, but in the light of the endowment of creation. He or she must examine in the same way the under-girding of any policy proposed. As so beautifully stated in the United States' Declaration of Independence:

> "...That whenever any Form of Government becomes destructive of these ends [the rights of "life liberty and the pursuit of happiness"] it is the Right of the People to alter or to abolish it, and to institute new Government... ...as to them shall seem most likely to effect their Safety and Happiness."

As people mature and come to direct their own lives, they also direct the lives of others to the extent that the country they live in allows them to participate in making its laws and influencing its customs. A total control by all of the people of these elements of living would occur in a perfect democracy. However, when humans examine and turn the forces of Gathering into laws or constitutions, they do not necessarily inculcate the best (read "sanest") ways for living, and usually get some things quite wrong.

For example, Democracy is not necessarily the answer to mankind's problems when some of the people of a "democracy" have enormous amounts of money, and the power that goes with such money, especially over the needy and the less educated.

Money and power, always substantive factors in human history, have gradually emerged in recent decades as capable of controlling the election process itself. The founding fathers, many of them quite wealthy, never dreamed of multi-billionaires whose private fortunes exceed that of many entire countries. They had no idea that, for example, ownership of media could manufacture consent to any idea that the owner wished to push forward, and do so just by clever advertising and by restricting the information allowed to get into the public's mind.

Plutocratic power-brokers spend an inordinate amount of time and money influencing politicians to gain laws that will enable them to do business without moral guidelines, and freedom from paying for their advantages. Their constant cry is "Deregulation!" unless a rule here or there will help them gain more money and power. For example, smog control devices may be welcomed on automobiles, but not on trucks or the smoke-stacks of industry.

Of course, these same plutocrats also want people to do the skilled labor required in their businesses and factories. Therefore, the propaganda in their newspapers continually trumpet the need for schools to prepare students for employment instead of for living. One great professor, when asked by some parents what their teenager should study at college, replied, "Have them teach him how to slay a dragon." Preparing for a job is called "Training." Preparing for life is called "Education" and, because of the many pitfalls on the road to a "good life", it requires knowledge of dragon-slaying. The main dragons are the temptations to getting "stuff" that really belongs to, or is needed by, others.

Democracy, since the time of the so-called Golden Age of Pericles (cir. 460-430 B.C.E.), has been held up as a cure for foolish kings, cruel czars, petty tyrants, and greedy dictators, but it was never thought to be a perfect answer. The founding fathers of the United States did not trust the vote of common people and set up a republic rather than a democracy. A democracy does not work unless the people voting on the issues are knowledgeable enough to distinguish the long term good of the people from the short term good of, say, a little more ready cash. When a few very rich men control almost all of the media and, through it, the details about the candidates for the people to elect the legislature, the long term good of the citizens can be hidden from the people.

As long ago as the 1830's, United States politics were channeled by those who had the power into a two-party system instead of a truly democratic free-for-all. The historian Howard Zinn has noted, "To give people a choice between two different parties and allow them, in a period of rebellion, to choose the slightly more democratic one was an ingenious method of control."[80] Any candidate, of course, not "approved" by the people with the real power, and the owners of the media, will never be heard from, or heard from so little that they will garner few votes. By 1911, Helen Keller would write to a suffragist in England, "Our democracy is but a name. We vote? What does that mean? It means that one choose between two bodies of real, though not avowed, autocrats. We choose between Tweedledum and Tweedledee."[81]

This situation is especially easy to maintain if the citizens' education can be weakened by under-funded schools and teachers. The resultant scene can be one in which persons approved by voters rush about the planet, even with large armies, under the guise of "making the world safe for democracies" while all the time seeking to set up republics or dictatorships that control the information and education that might create real democracies. Before the Vietnam War, Ho Chi Minh, the leader of North Vietnam, had only one desire, "to create a democracy like yours in the United States", as he wrote to the President of the United States and several congressmen. None of them

---

[80] Zinn, Howard, A People's History of the United States: 1492 – Present (Twentieth Anniversary Edition). Harper Collins: New York: 1999, p. 217. More than 700 pp., this is the only history book ever to sell over a million copies.
[81] Ibid., p.345.

answered him and the United States fought him so that it could reestablish the business-friendly colonial rule of France or, failing that, control the markets of Southeast Asia for United States businessmen.

The only answer to progress in today's world appears to be the education and maturation of so many people into being concerned with the world that the Order within them will steer them right past the "democratic" machinations of the greedy and power-mad. These latter notice this threat and, to no one's amazement, have made increasingly greater attacks on the funding of public schools.

Similarly, Capitalism has provided rules for doing business most effectively – but not necessarily what is best for the human race. Although favored by the media and most businessmen, Capitalism is not the way to develop the talents of the great masses of human beings called for by the apparent direction of our evolution. On the contrary, the developments most benefiting the average worker and his family have been those associations of persons who have fought against Capitalism the hardest – the Unions and the Socialists. Capitalism appears to be an excellent way to get an economy moving, but its natural direction (as Marx clearly pointed out) will lead it to a place where every capitalist will try to devour every other capitalist. The largest, most devouring one will be the final winner and owner of everything.

This self-aggrandizing path, strewn with the broken lives of those who trusted in it, is hardly the path of truth. The only things able to stop it are very strong laws. However, the constant cry of those who wish to keep it is, "Deregulation!" Regulation is decried as "Communist" and, of course, "against freedom." It is the latter, of course, if by "freedom" "license" is meant. The dissenting voices are left out by the media, primarily owned by capitalists.[82]

A prime example of how the powerful and wealthy generally inhibit the progress of a people can be seen in the world's so-called "War on Drugs." The latter was undertaken in spite of, and in the face of the absolutely disastrous failure of the war of the United States, known as "Prohibition," on the drug "alcohol." However, many rich and powerful people could become richer and more powerful if this "war" were undertaken. Like the "Cold War", wherein fortunes for the "military-industrial complex" were made arming the country against a mostly imaginary threat, the war on drugs made many new fortunes. Keeping out of the media the successes of the legalization and control of drugs by a few European countries, and placing false stories of their failure in the media, assured its establishment. The continuation of the war was assured when the thousands put into prison were discovered to be an excellent source of cheap labor for the powerful and their corporations. Why compete in the open labor market when you can get prison labor for twelve cents an hour? The building of new prisons goes on apace – well ahead of the building of schools – and prison systems are fast becoming gulag archipelagos of cheap labor.

The world budget for the War on Drugs grows and grows into many billions of dollars each year when the simple legalization like alcohol, with proper controls like alcohol, would eliminate immediately the entire problem

---

[82] In 2002, in America, according to economist Edward R. Wolff, the richest 1% of households owned 47% of the total wealth that exists! At this writing, 10% own 90%, and the gap is widening. People like the President Bush family, with over $400 millions, are commonplace among this group. Probably no one will ever hear the names of those who are in the top 1%, but that does not have any effect on their power.

of drug trafficking, and enormously downsize the general drug problem.[83] The silencing of the effective voices for this solution by the powerful, along with their continued pressing for more stories to indoctrinate the public to continue this clearly futile effort, is a problem that the progress of people appears powerless to solve – at least at present.[84]

A very great threat to the natural progress of a would-be healthy society, mentioned briefly above, is the private control of the media. When the information to a decision-making society is owned and operated by people whose wealth is enormous, the content of that media will never be permitted to criticize the greed of the enormously wealthy or their means of becoming that way. Moreover, when the primary means of becoming elected in a "democratic" country is through information given to a free society through the media, the elections as well as who runs for office can be controlled in the same way. No "Grand Conspiracy" theory needs to be invoked. The media, with hired hands slowly weeding out new employees who think differently than themselves, become mouthpieces of their owners. Main stream media are constantly making reference to their not being able to be influenced by "spin" and to their being interested only in the truth. But they carefully select each broadcaster, and thus subtly edit each broadcast.

The media have become so corrupt that interviewers and talk-show hosts have their guests and topics controlled. Many have discovered <u>after</u> their shows that this or that interviewee was allowed on the show only if they agreed to mention a certain product and/or brand name or medical

---

[83] In 2003, a professional survey showed that approximately three million people die every year from drugs. Of that number, 71% die from alcohol, 26% from tobacco-related drugs, and 3% from all other drugs combined. This throws into relief the actual futility of the War on Drugs.

[84] In 2002 reliable sources in California say that drugs were never more easily obtained than after many years of the "War on Drugs." Marijuana can now be obtained by any savvy person within twenty minutes of being requested for it, and cocaine within two hours. And the source-to-market time is dropping.

procedure. What you think you are seeing is not what you are getting. The people behind the scenes, and even sometimes on the scenes, have been paid, of course, to select the guests and arrange the agenda in a manner similar to the way they arrange the information at election times. No modern solution has been found to this problem, and present elections are almost farces.

The greatest threat to any society and the greatest corruption of the mystery of Gathering among persons, as follows naturally from what has already been said, would be the private gathering of the very wealthy to gain more wealth. This latter construct usually takes the form of a "Corporation."

What is not well known is that corporations were against the law as late as the 19th century and severely restricted in most of the twentieth century. They never really became legal.[85] But the corruption of greed, once entrenched, knows no bounds. Gradually the rich and powerful made corporations acceptable and, by control of information, made them regarded almost fondly by the public in some countries because of the alleged jobs they provided.[86] By the end of the 20th century their owners were anonymous, their locations international, their headquarters on foreign islands where they could not be taxed, and their machinations nefarious – and almost untouchable. They have all the rights of persons without any of the responsibilities. Through their control of the media, corporate critics are reviled and demonized, and even media news stories are chosen on the basis of "the bottom line" – profit. If a story criticizes too strongly the wishes of

---
[85] For the complete story of this travesty of justice in the United States, cf., Hartmann, Thom, Unequal Protection: The Rise of Corporate Dominance and the Theft of Human Rights. Rodale: St. Martin's Press, 2002.
[86] Professor Noam Chomsky of the Massachusettes Institute of Technology has often noted, "Wherever you read, 'Jobs! Jobs! Jobs!' read, 'Profits! Profits! Profits!'."

the owners, it is dropped from the next broadcast – if it ever makes it on – and the writer or announcer reprimanded and, in some cases, fired.

Spontaneous interviews and live broadcasts that contain elements the owners do not like – sometimes the most relevant items of the entire program – are edited out when rerun. Gaffs by persons in high government positions and industry, if admired by the owners, are removed from the records and history itself is rewritten. Persons in power, but disliked by the owners, have even their smallest errors magnified to the point of nausea. Sometimes they are simply lied about.

People standing for the dubious principles of the owners, sometimes even convicted felons or wanted for prosecution in foreign countries, are turned into media stars – and honest critics are never heard from. If grave concerns, like the steady collapse of a country's economy, might reflect badly on the owners' chosen leaders, insignificant but sensational side stories are kept dominant in the air time.

This enormous problem of modern society has no present solution because the very rich have for too long controlled the halls of power and have monopolized the positions of the lawmakers. By reason of a constant "selling" of the notions of rugged individualism rather than concern for "us", pursuit of wealth as a "good" thing rather than pursuit of maturity, a loving society in the "First World" is, at present, a dim prospect. Such societal behavior slows or entirely disrupts the obvious gatherings of Order in the procession of the equinoxes.[87]

---

[87] The classic text explaining the control of people by media-control is to be found in, Herman, Edward S. & Chomsky, Noam, <u>Manufacturing Consent: The Political Economy of the Mass Media</u>. Pantheon Books: New York, 1988 and 2002.

Perhaps the prime examples of the evils of corporations are that of a few debacles gaining publicity in the early 21st century. These corporations sometimes had little discernible production of anything. One primarily brokered the produce of others or of the Earth without any proportionate "production." In 1986, the "Business Plan" of this corporation, usually a document outlining the way production will be profitably managed, consisted almost solely in how to "influence" governments – local, state and federal – and through that influence receive the deregulation of its "produce", usually energy created by others. Free of the regulations and in control of most of the sources, it raised the prices of its commodity until its profits were astronomical. It succeeded in nearly bankrupting one of the United States, California, and several foreign countries, especially Argentina.

Similarly, another corporation acquired (and sold) the natural gas rights of Bolivia, and another corporation acquired most of the water rights of the same country. The people of Cochabamba awoke one morning to discover that they owned none of the water in the area of their city and the cost of water was beyond their means. They did what people have done throughout history – they rebelled in riots. The army was called in because the corporation, of course, had "influenced" the rulers of the country to let them acquire the water rights. The people held out anyway and, after a number were killed, they kept their own water.

A danger to humankind related to the corporations just mentioned is the new notion of "Imperialism" afoot in the world. Imperialism once meant the domination of weaker countries by larger ones, the latter using armies to conquer the weak and make them colonies. As colonies, a major part of their wealth was systematically drained away to the Imperial Power. In the twenty-first century this has taken a new turn. The stronger power does not bother to expend money on armies to conquer the weaker country. Rather it bribes a powerful group already in the country with money and arms, and helps them take over. Then, deals are made with the new rulers insuring the same drain of wealth to the Imperial Power behind the throne. Dictators are preferred. The whole ugly mess is sometimes disguised under the name, "Globalization."[88]

The obvious struggle going on in the world between human development towards Order and the development of human greed towards chaos is quite instructive for the person seeking the Meaning of Life. Comparing two countries, the USA and the Massai tribe, is helpful. The position of the United States, the largest source of *laissez faire* capitalists in the society of the world, is becoming one of a pariah. It uses its military to protect its overseas investments, disguising them as "national interests." Of the more than two hundred "interventions" by United States military in the last fifty years, almost all have been carried out in the name of "National Security." They have caused the deaths of tens of thousands of innocent persons in many places, dismissed under the notion of "collateral damage", and the US, along with Israel, Iraq, and maybe China, has become the most hated nation in the world.[89] The names of these "interventions" are great examples of what was referred to above as "media control." They are always quite noble or patriotic sounding, like "Supply Hope", "Provide Hope", "Vigilant Sentinel", or "Constant Vigil." But they kill just as many people as do the ones with more vicious sobriquets like, "Urgent Fury", the title used when,

---

[88] For interesting views, cf. Michael Czerny, "University and Globalization: Yes, But", and, Stackhouse, Max , Globilization, Public Theology, and New Means of Grace. The Santa Clara Lectures, Vol.9, #1, November, 2002, and #2, January, 2003. www.scu.edu/BannanCenter
[89] Cf. esp. Gore Vidal, Perpetual War for Perpetual Peace: How We Got To Be So Hated. Nation Books: New York, 2002.

under Commander-in-Chief Ronald Reagan, the American forces were victorious in their invasion of that terribly threatening, island-country of Grenada. If other people's opinion has any weight at all, the United States is not making much progress towards mature humanity.

In contrast to this our cousins, the leaders and people of the Massai tribe in Africa, show a much different level of progress. Those people live in a very simple society and more than six months passed after the terrifying disaster of the towers in New York on 9/11/01 before they were able to grasp what had happened by getting pictures. Having no knowledge of the vastness and riches of the United States, they immediately took up a collection of their most valuable possessions, cattle, and offered a small herd to the United States to help them in their misery. Estimates of the value of the gift compared to the total worth of the Massai tribe indicate that the relative value of a gift by the US in US currency would be in the neighborhood of one trillion dollars! Prospects of maturation for the Massai and their leaders would seem to be at a very high level.

Such has been a few of the developmental paths of humans using their knowledge and science. Human beings definitely affect the unfolding of the Cosmos, and set directions for the course of history. Historians generally agree that Rome destroyed itself gradually, from within. Considering the number and destructive power of atomic bombs made by those who have the capacity, the total annihilation of the human race by the human race is definitely now possible.

Obviously, the choices of humans affect their future, both as individuals and as societies. The atmosphere created by the media – some of ourselves – clearly makes a difference in the lives of the people so that their character, their history and the length of their lives are deeply affected. And certainly if a few mad members of the race can annihilate us all, then our future, whether developed through the Cosmic Laws of Gathering, Centering, and Internalizing or through our own efforts, is in our hands. We are all in this together, whether we like it or not. But does human decision change the <u>nature</u> of man?

We launch into speculation. Some very respectable scientists say that the age and size of the Universe since the Incomprehensible Explosion indicates the number of worlds like our own to be in the neighborhood of many more than 50,000. None are reachable by any presently known means, even to communicate with. The nearest world, much further away than the nearest star which is a few light years distant, would be so far away that the speed of the communication impulse – the speed of light – would leave the sender a bit bored of the whole process, and probably dead, before a message could be received and sent back. We had best, for practical purposes, consider ourselves to be alone until we find real evidence of the "warp" in time that exists presently only in theories of "cosmic strings"[90] or science fiction.

But somewhere a world might exist burnt to a cinder by overzealous warriors with atomic bombs. Then again, somewhere a world might exist filled to the brim with peaceful citizens, loving and caring for each other. Perhaps the moment they all bow and acknowledge the Someone together they would cause the creation of the next Phase – a Union of Minds together with the Someone who authored the whole business, the Noosphere of Teilhard de Chardin, the heaven of Christianity and some other religions. *Oremus pro invicem ("Let us pray for one another")*.

---

[90] Magueijo, Faster...., pp.228-229.

SUMMARY

I,i. Beginning: All that is contained in the physical universe came from an enormous explosion a long time ago.

I,ii. Order: The explosion was very orderly from its beginning, and everything we know about flowed very precisely from the explosion.

I,iii. The Questions: What we want to know is, "Why did the explosion occur?" This question is not a physical or psychological question, but an ultimate, philosophical one, namely, "Why are we?"

I,iv. Laws: The orderly manner of the explosion is the result of Laws that are found in the developing universe and are inherent in the many parts of the universe.

I,v. Things: The effect of the laws inherent in the explosion was the unfolding of a great variety of things from galaxies with suns and planets, to at least one very orderly planet, Earth, with a biosphere filled with different things, living and non-living.

I,vi. Humans: Living things on Earth emerged and became more complex and centered until one, *homo sapiens sapiens*, evolved with the ability to think both concretely and abstractly, to make all kinds of investigations, and eventually form orderly bodies of learning, schools, and universities. A non-material center, called a "soul", seems to have evolved for this creature, and it holds and uses the abstract material of learning. It appears to be made of Dark Matter and Dark Energy.

A very important fact about this new creature, man, was its ability to choose freely. What had been an automatic unfolding from the explosion could now be altered by the choices of humans. This thinking being, able to choose the good of others over the self, to love, could blossom into a very admirable creature – or not.

Love is the highest form of human activity and becoming one who loves transforms the human into a "person." The ability to exercise love by a human does not happen automatically, unlike the acquisition of that power. Loving is the result of gradual growth and maturation, sometimes does not happen at all, and sometimes stops far short of being true and disinterested. What research seems to establish is that the human being needs to examine all the evidence of its own orderly environment, become wise from it, and then become a good, loving person

I,vii. Someone: The greatest discoveries of the thinking humans were about their own origin, when and how it occurred, and that it occurred by the efforts of Someone. This Someone we call "God." God must have been responsible for the explosion, and have all the attributes of the evolved material, but in a superior manner, beyond our comprehension.

I,viii. Spirituality: A personal relation with the Author of the first explosion, the Originator, or "God", is called "Spirituality" and a person with a real relation with God is called a "spiritual person." All humans have the possibility to be spiritual by acknowledging God and asking for directions for their personal gift of life. The onset of a spirituality is most evident in addiction-recovery programs.

I,ix. Spiritual Development: Persons grow in spirituality by developing whatever talents they have and by putting them at the service of others, that is, by loving them. Even with the best intentions, humans err in their choices to be loving unless they listen to the promptings of Order within them, called "prayer." To pray is to listen to Order – to the God Who made people able to listen and holds them in existence. If what is "heard" leads to love, peace, joy, harmony, and such like, following it will lead to an ever greater spirituality. Humans have great difficulty doing this.

I,x. Meaning: The meaning of life, derived from the gradual and increasing complexity of the things emerging from the initial explosion, the Big Bang, is to love. Apparently originating from a act of sharing life, an act of love by the Originator, the developed human reaches perfection by imitating the Originator and loving as well as possible. To understand this meaning and to live it is wisdom, the goal of life.

I,xi. Death and Life: The frustration of human death is an anomaly that flies in the face of the orderly unfolding that culminated in humans, and the loving relating and gatherings that occur among loving humans. The only reasonable solution is that death is a passage to another life, not an end. We know little about this new realm, but clues in this life hint at a "place" where gathering, loving, and even relating to God can occur.

I,xii. Conclusion: Life is a gift and a mystery to be lived. It contains all the clues needed for getting directions, and to find them is wisdom. Its goal, for each unique human, is to become as loving as possible and be like the One Who gave the gift. However, few people, and only after a long time, and with many errors mixed in, ever seem able to find their way to its meaning.

Part II: Most of Christianity is in complete sympathy with all that has been derived about life from the clues available. However, acting on faith in Jesus of Nazareth–especially by trusting in the sacred writings about him–Christianity has struggled for centuries to fill in many of the pieces missing from the puzzle of life, and provides many places to look for other missing pieces. Its belief in the Trinity provides a model, and fits hand-in-glove with the basic laws of the universe, Gathering and Centering. It also provides a motive for everything coming to be–God's love. This love, Christianity says, is God. Christianity, built on a gift of Faith, is necessary for humans because the rational order, laid out in this book as found by Science, and leading to God, is far too complicated and difficult for people given the shortness of life. Faith is necessary.

Part III: The method used to arrive at the conclusions of this treatise is one of induction from effects to causes, much the way the atom was discovered and described. Similar to the way a criminal is described, typed, and found out by clues at a crime scene, the meaning of life is extracted from the scene of the gift of human life, and the evolutionary way that gift was delivered to us. The meaning of life is not only discoverable by such methods, but the Source of Life, the Original Orderer, is also discovered in this way.

Part IV: The story of mankind trying to make sense of life is a rather pathetic one. Emerging out of eons of competition, humans basically miss the meaning of life as love, and try to turn it to their personal advantage, chiefly by exercising power or shrewd commerce in a very self-centered way. The result is that everyone around them must struggle constantly to survive or else slip into terrible hardship. The final result is to make life for many look less like a gift than a curse, with those enjoying abundance reinforcing that view. A basic conversion to a view that love is the meaning of life, and that wisdom is to be preferred to wealth, seems necessary.

Dark Matter and the Soul

In August of 2006, the world welcomed the news of the proof of the existence of Dark Matter. Almost immediately, many scientists rushed to question the conclusion, even going so far as to modify Newton's second law of motion to explain the discrepancies that caused its positing. The controversy arose because of a "mismatch in the masses of galaxies and large cosmic structures." Enormous masses were missing and left unexplained – or at least, that is what scientists are claiming. If the disequilibrium is caused by anything other than Dark Mass, science is not willing to admit it.

More recently, a feature article in <u>Scientific American</u> (March, 2010) discussed Dark Energy as the possible source of a multitude of thought-processing in the brain's DMN (Default Mode Network). The laboratory doing the testing found them unaccounted for by the measured output of energy.

The original positing of Dark Matter/Energy was an inference from phenomena clearly observed. Like the atom before it, Dark Matter remained a theory for many years. (This author grew up with the "atomic theory", not the "atomic fact." At the destruction of Hiroshima, the whole world started thinking differently.) Like atoms, Dark Matter and Energy are now clearly imposing themselves into explanations of mysterious phenomena.

We are concerned here with the reasoning process as well as the conclusions of this scientific investigation because of the implications for the traditional notion of "soul." To philosophers, the peculiar thing about the positing of Dark Matter/Energy was the allowance of the positing at all. Atoms had had a slightly different history; they had to be *seen* before becoming truly factual rather than theoretical. Even after Hiroshima, but before the electron microscope was invented, no one seemed to question the existence of atoms. Nonetheless, the epithet "Atomic Theory" persisted because they had never been seen, heard, felt, tasted or smelled. Since the 2006 announcement, no one has ever yet observed any Dark Matter. However, the changes in matter that *were* observed, now seem to justify the positing of it anyway.

Why is the phenomenon of a shortage of mass or energy permission for positing something unknown when far more obvious phenomena do not give such permission? Many different phenomena remain unexplained that are observed everyday, from the action of molecular changes to the formation of theories of relativity in the minds of physicists. The traditional attempts to posit the kinds of material that might explain these phenomena, immaterial souls, have been quickly rejected as "unscientific." Something is amiss here.

The best method for dealing with the world around us has come to be The Scientific Method. Arguing from Observation and controlled Experimentation, it moves to Theory and then to Law. From the known laws, it can then extrapolate from ever-increasing data, primarily using mathematics, until a great deal even about distant galaxies can be explained. Items not available to observation and experimentation are deemed to be "unscientific", and must be held to be "merely theoretical" for purposes of modern science. This is not to say they do not, or cannot, exist; but they must remain theories. That is why the scientific claims of "proof" of Dark Matter and Dark Energy are such an oddity.

Some people probably welcomed the 2006 announcement. For instance, the spirits of many ancient philosophers must have leapt happily in the realm of the dead – if one exists. With 23% of the Universe computed to be Dark Matter and 70% Dark Energy, Plato's stout claim of existence of the Forms moved forward a notch. Let us examine the source of Plato's probable enthusiasm with an example.

Microscopic animals, like the amoeba, do amazing things that are quite unexplained by zoologists. These scientists readily tell us *what* they do, but they avoid telling us how they can possibly do it. Their feeding, for example, is described thus:

"The amoeba eats other protozoans, algae, rotifers, and dead protoplasm, preferring small, live flagellates and ciliates. It may eat several paramecia or several hundred small flagellates daily and exhibits choice in selecting food. The amoeba is attracted by movements of the intended prey or by substances diffusing from it; unwanted or indigestible materials are usually avoided, as are organisms that show intense activity. Food may be taken in at any part of the cell surface. The amoeba extends pseudopodia that encircle the food which, with some water, is taken into the endoplasm as a food vacuole. More water is included with an active item than with one that is quiet. The vacuoles are moved about by streaming movements in the endoplasm and thus come in contact with various parts of it. A recently formed vacuole gives an acid reaction, probably because of a secretion that kills the prey quickly. … The vacuoles decrease in size as digestion proceeds, and any undigested residues are egested by being passed to the outside at any place on the cell surface." (Storer, Tracy I., General Zoology, McGraw-Hill, New York, 1951, p. 277.)

If Plato read that passage, his first question to himself would have been, "How could that animal know how to do all that?" Especially if he knew they had but a single cell, he would probably have said, "My, those amoebae really participate in an interesting Form." Aristotle would have said, "What a complex soul for such a small animal!" Naturally, no mention of "form" or "soul" would be found in the zoology textbook. Neither man would have accepted an answer that claimed that the quantified parts did the feeding all by themselves. Having quantity was, for them, an extremely limiting feature of any being.

I would like to suggest that the scientific and philosophic approaches are both correct. Limited to the Scientific Method and measurable and observable phenomena, the textbook has no business discussing souls. Nonetheless, after the activity is described in great detail, the complex, unified effort of the amoeba remains subject to some quite legitimate questions. "How do its parts work together to feed?" "How does it know how to feed?" "What moves its pseudopodia in the direction of the food?" The same kinds of questions are natural to all living things, even to a human being who is obviously far more complex.

No observable material offers an answer to these questions. To say God or angels did the movements is pure guessing. Nor will it do to say that one part moved the others if that part is also a product of a prior movement of the same being. The unifying force of a living thing is not the result or product of its parts, but is prior to them and the only possible source of their formation. Such a source, called a soul, must be the director of their unified development – including the dramatic metamorphoses of caterpillars to butterflies.

A "soul"? The fact that more and more quantified bits of stuff are added to the amoeba by itself – the phenomenon we call "growth" – would also prevent any other answer. This is especially true when the bits of stuff, once just dead animals or bits of algae, are now totally engaged in a unified effort of the amoeba (we might call him "Slinky") to catch new meals.

The overwhelming evidence is that the amoeba fed itself, and its unified activity has a central director. It has a "soul", and the soul is "Dark." The soul of the amoeba may have a different kind of knowledge from humans, but it is aware of food around it, moves towards it, ingests and digests it, and egests the leftovers. Every atom of the one-celled amoeba is under the control of itself, and without any nerves. The soul or form of the amoeba enabling it to do these things is just "stuff", but it is Dark, immensely complex, and quite wonderful in its achievement.

Plato would have described the form of the amoeba as an existent of a world we cannot see except like shadows on a wall. When we see shadows, we can know something about whatever made the shadow, and sometimes a great deal. However, we cannot come close to what we could know in a direct encounter. For Plato, the individual beings of our daily experience are bits of quantity that, being indefinite in themselves, become a "something" by participating – a kind of 'reflecting' – in the much more real, Dark World of Forms. Plato would have been greatly puzzled by the discovery of Dark Matter.

Aristotle would have described the soul of the amoeba as its "form", a technical term for its "whatness." But he would have the form exist in each amoeba as a Dark principle of its being, and not a mere reflection of a more real world elsewhere. The soul/form would have the ability to grasp the atoms within the amoeba and unify them into a single existent. As the amoeba reproduced by dividing, the Dark form would divide also. The new forms would direct the organizations of the parts of new amoebae, as well as control their ongoing movement, feeding, growth, and reproduction.

Humans would be treated in a similar manner to amoebae, though their souls would be of a far more complex kind. For humans, for example, look at the process of healing in a child with a lacerated, broken arm. The body goes to work on both. If a doctor sets the bone, in a year or so absolutely no sign might exist of the trauma. Bone, sinew, soft tissue, all work in harmony in a manner that remains totally unexplained. All of the parts of the process can be measured. Slow motion cameras can even record the soft tissue kneading together and, in many cases, completely erasing any signs of the trauma. Much of the procedure happens while the child is asleep, and none of it is understood by the child or explainable by even the most astute physician. Such unified complexities do not happen by themselves. They also cease immediately if death occurs. Some center of the child directs the whole business – and it is Dark. May it be called the child's "soul"?

Plato's human soul, a 'reflecting' of the Form, "Human", in the more real "World of Forms", would be like a rider on a horse, directing all of the quantified-into-space human activities. When the human died, the body would lose its participation in the form and the soul would rejoin the World of Forms, now specified by its history. It might even come back to Earth again, directing a new body. Dark Matter would have been something like a mirror for Plato.

For Aristotle, the act of understanding was performed by the soul alone and not merely without quantity, but *repugnant* to quantity. At least in acts of understanding, the human soul could somehow live by itself when detached from its body. It might well be able to do other things as well. After all, this understanding soul is the same soul that grasped the stuff of the fertilized ovum and formed it into a body that could live outside the Mother, and with no help from the Mother except as a host. The obvious problem here for both Plato and

Aristotle is that they had no simply existing "stuff", like Dark Matter, with which to explain the many phenomena that living human beings exhibit.

Thomas Aquinas ran into this same problem while examining the make-up of the soul of man. In the <u>Summa Theologica</u>, he had to face the objection that

> "…things which have no matter, have no cause of their existence, as the Philosopher says (VIII Metaph.). But the soul has a cause of its existence, since it is created by God. Therefore, the soul has matter." (<u>Summa Theologica</u>, q.75, a.4, obj.3.)

In his answer, Thomas knew only of quantified matter in human bodies and also knew it was repugnant to the act of understanding. He cleverly quotes Aristotle, "the Philosopher", as saying that things that have no matter are simply "beings at once." This meant they could simply "be", complete and fully as single beings. They obviously had no matter, or they would be discovered, be visible, heard, or some such.

Not having the powerful, dynamic kind of being of Dark Matter with Dark Energy, these philosophers were limited to one kind of "act" or "form." They also had only one kind of quantified matter in the things of this world: three-dimensional matter. The "angels" of Thomas and the "separated substances" of Aristotle had no matter in them. This reduced each one of them to being a complete species in itself – one of a kind.

Living things of Earth were different. Though limited by quantity in time and space, the quantity enabled them to become individuals of the same species and to increase and multiply as far as the environment would sustain them. As they became understanding, at least that part of them could operate without matter. If they survived death, they would need a body for any kind of really human life. St. Thomas, of course, being a Dominican monk, simply ascribed to the creedal notion of the "resurrection of the body." But it is a "glorified" body, and quite a step up from the base, quantified body of daily life. After all, he noted, when Christ arose from the dead, He could come into the room where the Apostles were, "the doors being shut." He could eat with them – and ascend into Heaven. In many ways, the risen Christ sounds mostly like a Dark "Force" that organized its body in the womb of the Blessed Mother.

Picture these ancient thinkers in a modern world where an immense range of Dark Matter might exist. Things can be differentiated within themselves in a manner unknown to those great minds of the past. Powerful "centers" of "stuff" can form single things out of what is around them. They probably exist in great numbers in different atoms, molecules, and living things.

The great theologian-philosopher of the last century, Karl Rahner, ran into a similar problem of unexplained phenomena. He took another look at one of the central philosophical questions of all times, "Can the existence of anything beyond measurable and observable phenomena be proven?" Another way of asking this is, "Is metaphysics possible?" He tried a new tack. His doctoral dissertation, "Spirit in the World" (Geist in Welt) is a tour-de-force aimed at establishing that, though limited in origin to our sense knowledge of things in the world, human knowing goes beyond our senses to the very being of things outside us. That is why we can say something "*is*." His word, "spirit" (German, "Geist"), is chosen to indicate anything that is not measurable or observable – not scientific. He ends up asserting that we could not have known of the "existence" of things outside our bodies unless more came into our minds than the mere light-waves or sound-waves that brought the outside world into us. To judge, at least with any semblance of truth, that an object outside us "is" goes beyond the measurable and observable. "Is" simply is not sensible, but "only" intellectual. "Is" – existence – is everywhere, knowable, and able to be judged affirmatively, but it is not able to be sensed.

What if, when he did his work in 1935, Rahner had proof of Dark Matter with Dark Energy? Would he have said "Dark Matter in the World" instead of "Spirit in the World"? "Dunkelstoff" instead of "Geist"? Would the scientists have complained that you may posit an explanation for the missing mass of things, but not any other phenomena? Do not our claim of truth and our search for truth require far more that we posit an explanation for the existence, unity and activity of things than for the mass of a galaxy? If, indeed, we have souls that are a Dark, intrinsic part of each human being – some material that can understand and reason apart from their bodies – cultivating them might be more widely accepted.

Here is a good place to summarize the thoughts on souls of Wilder Penfield, M.D., a Canadian surgeon, as reported by Melvin Morse, M.D. (Closer to the Light: Learning from Children's Near Death Experiences, 1990). Dr. Penfield is known as "The Father of Neuroscience." He is the man who did the first mapping of the brain, pinpointing which parts of the brain controlled which movements of the body. For most of his life he did not believe in the existence of the soul, primarily because it was not measurable or observable. He went so far as to illustrate his disbelief by painting an illustration of it on a large rock in a field of his farm. He put the Greek world for "spirit" on one side of the rock, and the outline of a human head on the other with a question mark where the brain should be. He connected the two with a solid line and to the accepted image of the science of Medicine, the Aesculapian Torch. This meant to him that Medicine had answered all of the questions about minds and bodies.

Fifty years later, he changed his opinion. Deeply concerned about his new insight, he bundled up his aged body in "six sweaters" to ward off the Canadian winter, went out, and repainted the rock. He crossed out the solid line and replaced it with a dotted line and a question mark. He later wrote, "I came to take seriously, even to believe, that the consciousness of man, the mind, is NOT something to be reduced to brain mechanism." He also expressed the sentiments of Aristotle that this search is "perhaps the most difficult and most important of all problems."

Our souls are obviously dependent for their initial knowledge on the five senses encountering regular matter. However, if souls were commonly accepted to be of real, Dark Matter/Energy that reaches through the sense data and grasps the truth of the Universe, more respect for life itself might be engendered. That would be a pleasant change.

www.ingramcontent.com/pod-product-compliance
Lightning Source LLC
Chambersburg PA
CBHW051409070526
44584CB00023B/3360